OXFORD **IB PREPARED**

HISTORY

IB DIPLOMA PROGRAMME

David M. Smith

Sheta Saha

OXFORD **IB PREPARED**

OXFORD
UNIVERSITY PRESS

OXFORD
UNIVERSITY PRESS

Great Clarendon Street, Oxford, OX2 6DP, United Kingdom

Oxford University Press is a department of the University of Oxford. It furthers the University's objective of excellence in research, scholarship, and education by publishing worldwide. Oxford is a registered trade mark of Oxford University Press in the UK and in certain other countries

British Library Cataloguing in Publication Data
Data available

978-0-19-843428-3

10 9 8 7 6 5 4 3 2 1

Paper used in the production of this book is a natural, recyclable product made from wood grown in sustainable forests. The manufacturing process conforms to the environmental regulations of the country of origin.

Printed in India by Manipal Technologies Limited

Acknowledgements

Photo credits:

Cover image: Tetra Images/Alamy Stock Photo; **p1:** badahos/ Shutterstock; **p3:** Bettmann/Getty Images; **pp9, 26:** Punch Cartoon Library/TopFoto; **p31:** Everett Historical / Shutterstock; **p60:** powerofforever/iStock/Getty Images Plus; **p130:** David Low/Solo Syndication dmg media/British Cartoon Archive, University of Kent.

Artwork by Q2A Media Services Pvt. Ltd.

The publisher would like to thank the International Baccalaureate for their kind permission to adapt questions from past examinations and content from the subject guide. The questions adapted for this book, and the corresponding past paper references, are summarized here:

Question practice, **p2:** M17 BP1 TZ0 Q17(a) and (b), Q18, Q19, Q20; Question practice, **pp3–4:** M17 BP1 TZ0 Sources MNOP; Question practice, **pp8–9:** N17 BP1 TZ0 Sources IJKL, Q9(a) and (b); Figure 1.3.1, **p11:** M17 BP1 TZ0 Source M; Example, **p13:** M17 BP1 TZ0 Q18; Question practice, **p14:** N17 BP1 TZ0 Source M, Q14; Question practice, **p16:** M17 BP1 TZ0 Q11, N17 BP1 TZ0 Q11; Question practice, **pp17–18:** N17 BP1 TZ0 Sources BC, Q3; Example, **p20:** N17 BP1 TZ0 Q4; Example, **p21:** M17 BP1 TZ0 Q9; Question practice, **p23:** N17 BP1 TZ0 Q12; Question practice, **pp24–6:** N17 BP1 TZ0 Sources IJKL, Q9(a) and (b), Q10, Q11, Q12; Question practice, **p33:** M17 BP2 TZ0 Q11, Q12, Q13, Q14; Figure 2.2.1, **p35:** M17 BP2 TZ0 Q15; Example (top), **p35:** M17 BP2 TZ0 Q9; Example (bottom), **p35:** N18 BP2 TZ0 Q23; Example, **p36:** N17 BP2 TZ0 Q13; Example, **p37:** N17 BP2 TZ0 Q22; Question practice, **p37:** N17 BP2 TZ0 Q19; Question practice, **p39:** N17 BP2 TZ0 Q2, Q3, Q15, Q17, Q21, Q24; Question practice, **p39:** N17 BP2 TZ0 Q21; Question practice, **p43:** M17 BP2 TZ0 Q22; Question practice, **p46:** N17 BP2 TZ0 Q23; Example, **p50:** N17 BP2 TZ0 Q19; Question practice, **p52:** N17 BP2 TZ0 Q19; Question practice, **p57:** N17 BP2 TZ0 Q23; Concept link, **p63:** M18 HP3 TZ0 Q28, Q25; Assessment tip, **p64:** N17 HP3 TZ0 Q35, Q33; Example,

p65: M18 HP3 TZ0 Q27, Q28; Question practice, **p66:** M17 HP3 TZ0 Q15, Q16; Question practice, **p69:** M17 HP3 TZ0 Q23; Assessment tip, **p70:** N17 HP3 TZ0 Q23; Question practice, **p70:** N17 HP3 TZ0 Q16; Question practice, **p76:** N17 HP3 TZ0 Q29; Question practice, **p80:** M18 HP3 TZ0 Q33; Question practice, **p85:** N17 HP3 TZ0 Q34; Question practice, **p90:** N17 HP3 TZ0 Q25; Question practice, **p94:** M18 HP3 TZ0 Q20; Question practice, **p98:** N17 HP3 TZ0 Q23; Question practice, **p102:** N17 HP3 TZ0 Q18; Question practice, **p106:** M18 HP3 TZ0 Q28; Question practice, **p110:** N17 HP3 TZ0 Q29; Question practice, **p114:** N17 HP3 TZ0 Q23; Question practice, **p118:** N17 HP3 TZ0 Q26.

The authors and publisher are grateful to those who have given permission to reproduce the following extracts and adaptations of copyright material:

Beasley, William: excerpt from *Japanese Imperialism, 1894-1945* by William Beasley (1987), Oxford University Press, Inc. New York, © W. G. Beasley 1987, reproduced with permission of the Licensor through PLSclear.

Brady, Tom: a judge and a leader of the pro-segregation White Citizens' Council movement, writing about his speech to the Indianola Citizens' Council in his pamphlet 'A Review of Black Monday', 28 October 1954 (The University of Southern Mississippi, Collection M393).

Daily Express/Express Syndication: excerpt from an editorial in the Daily Express, 30 September, 1938, reproduced by permission.

Guardian News & Media Ltd: excerpt from an editorial in the *The Manchester Guardian*, a British newspaper, 1 October, 1938, copyright Guardian News & Media, Ltd., reproduced by permission.

Jackson, Peter: excerpt from The Mongols and the West, 1221–1410, Routledge, 2014, © 2005 Taylor & Francis, reproduced by permission of Taylor & Francis Group, permission conveyed through Copyright Clearance Center, Inc.

Klarman, M: excerpt from *Brown v Board of Education and the Civil Rights Movement*, copyright © 2007 by Oxford University Press, Inc., New York, Oxford University Press, reproduced with permission of the Licensor through PLSclear.

Lu, David J.: excerpt from *Japan: a Documentary History*, M. E. Sharpe 1996, © 2005 by David J Lu, reproduced with permission of Taylor & Francis Group, permission conveyed through Copyright Clearance Center, Inc.

Overy, Richard: excerpt from 'Soviet Union' from *The Road to War: Revised Edition* by Richard Overy with Andrew Wheatcroft, copyright © 1989, 1999 by Richard Overy & Andrew Wheatcroft, reproduced by permission of Penguin Random House UK and Viking Books, an imprint of Penguin Publishing Group, a division of Penguin Random House LLC, all rights reserved.

van de Ven, Hans: excerpt from *War and Nationalism in China: 1925–1945*, RoutledgeCurzon, 2003, © 2003 Hans J. van de Ven, reproduced by permission of Taylor & Francis Group, permission conveyed through Copyright Clearance Center, Inc.

Weatherford, Jack: excerpt 'War of the Khans' from *Genghis Khan and the Making of the Modern World*, copyright © 2004 by Jack Weatherford, reproduced by permission of Crown Books, an imprint of Random House, a division of Penguin Random House LLC, all rights reserved.

Sources:

Moynihan, Daniel Patrick: a former US Navy officer and a sociologist who was Assistant Secretary of Labor for President Lyndon B Johnson, writing in the report 'The Negro Family: The Case for National Action' (March 1965).

Records of the Supreme Court of the United States: Brown v. Board of Education of Topeka, Kansas, May 17, 1954, Records of the Supreme Court of the United States, Record Group 267, National Archives.

Although every effort has been made to trace and contact copyright holders before publication, this has not been possible in some cases. We apologise for any apparent infringement of copyright and if notified, the publisher will be pleased to rectify any errors or omissions at the earliest opportunity.

Links to third party websites are provided by Oxford in good faith and for information only. Oxford disclaims any responsibility for the materials contained in any third party website referenced in this work.

Contents

Answers to the practice exam paper questions in this book can be found on your free support website. Access the support website here:

www.oxfordsecondary.com/ib-prepared-support

INTRODUCTION

This book provides a guide to preparing for International Baccalaureate history assessments. This includes your internal assessment and your external assessment. In the following chapters, you will find the essential concepts and skills needed to be successful in these assessments. There are tips for preparing for and sitting the exams, as well as past exam questions on which to practise in each chapter. You can check your answers against markschemes as well as annotated student samples. The last chapter has a set of exam-style questions so you can check your preparation for the exams against the markshemes at: **www.oxfordsecondary.com/ib-prepared-support.**

Assessment in IB history

All IB courses have assessments that are assessed by external examiners (external assessments) and assessments that are assessed by your teachers (internal assessments). In IB history, the external assessments consist of three papers. The internal assessment is a historical investigation. If you are studying the standard level IB history course, you will complete paper 1 (prescribed subject), paper 2 (world history topics), and the historical investigation. If you are studying the higher level, you will also complete paper 3 (regional option). The weighting is as follows:

Standard level

Component	Options	Weighting
Paper 1	1 prescribed subject	30%
Paper 2	2 world history topics	45%
Internal assessment		25%

Higher level

Component	Options	Weighting
Paper 1	1 prescribed subject	20%
Paper 2	2 world history topics	25%
Paper 3	3 sections of a regional option	35%
Internal assessment		20%

Based on these assessments, you will be awarded a mark out of 7 for IB history:

Grade	Descriptor
7	Demonstrates conceptual awareness, insight, and knowledge and understanding which are evident in the skills of critical thinking; a high level of ability to provide answers which are fully developed, structured in a logical and coherent manner and illustrated with appropriate examples; a precise use of terminology which is specific to the subject; familiarity with the literature of the subject; the ability to analyse and evaluate evidence and to synthesize knowledge and concepts; awareness of alternative points of view and subjective and ideological biases, and the ability to come to reasonable, albeit tentative, conclusions; consistent evidence of critical reflective thinking; a high level of proficiency in analysing and evaluating data or problem solving.
6	Demonstrates detailed knowledge and understanding; answers which are coherent, logically structured and well developed; consistent use of appropriate terminology; an ability to analyse, evaluate and synthesize knowledge and concepts; knowledge of relevant research, theories and issues, and awareness of different perspectives and contexts from which these have been developed; consistent evidence of critical thinking; an ability to analyse and evaluate data or to solve problems competently.
5	Demonstrates a sound knowledge and understanding of the subject using subject-specific terminology; answers which are logically structured and coherent but not fully developed; an ability to provide competent answers with some attempt to integrate knowledge and concepts; a tendency to be more descriptive than evaluative although some ability is demonstrated to present and develop contrasting points of view; some evidence of critical thinking; an ability to analyse and evaluate data or to solve problems.
4	Demonstrates a secure knowledge and understanding of the subject going beyond the mere citing of isolated, fragmentary, irrelevant or "common sense" points; some ability to structure answers but with insufficient clarity and possibly some repetition; an ability to express knowledge and understanding in terminology specific to the subject; some understanding of the way facts or ideas may be related and embodied in principles and concepts; some ability to develop ideas and substantiate assertions; use of knowledge and understanding which is more descriptive than analytical; some ability to compensate for gaps in knowledge and understanding through rudimentary application or evaluation of that knowledge; an ability to interpret data or to solve problems and some ability to engage in analysis and evaluation.
3	Demonstrates some knowledge and understanding of the subject; a basic sense of structure that is not sustained throughout the answers; a basic use of terminology appropriate to the subject; some ability to establish links between facts or ideas; some ability to comprehend data or to solve problems.
2	Demonstrates a limited knowledge and understanding of the subject; some sense of structure in the answers; a limited use of terminology appropriate to the subject; a limited ability to establish links between facts or ideas; a basic ability to comprehend data or to solve problems.
1	Demonstrates very limited knowledge and understanding of the subject; almost no organizational structure in the answers; inappropriate or inadequate use of terminology; a limited ability to comprehend data or to solve problems.

Command terms

Command terms are the portion of a question that describes the nature of the task you are being asked to do. It is important to understand exactly what each of these terms requires, as they form the basis of the assessment of your responses. In other words, to do well, it is important to understand exactly what the question is asking. The following is a list of the command terms used in IB history assessments.

Command term	Definition
Analyse	Break down in order to bring out the essential elements or structure.
Compare	Give an account of the similarities between two (or more) items or situations, referring to both (all) of them.
Compare and contrast	Give an account of similarities and differences between two (or more) items or situations, referring to both (all) of them throughout.
Contrast	Give an account of the differences between two (or more) items or situations, referring to both (all) of them.
Discuss	Offer a considered and balanced review that includes a range of arguments, factors or hypotheses. Opinions or conclusions should be presented clearly and supported by appropriate evidence.
Evaluate	Make an appraisal by weighing up the strengths and limitations.
Examine	Consider an argument or concept in a way that uncovers the assumptions and interrelationships of the issue.
To what extent	Consider the merits or otherwise of an argument or concept. Opinions and conclusions should be presented clearly and supported with appropriate evidence and sound argument.

Source: IB History guide

Book structure

This book is divided into chapters that correspond to the four elements of assessment in IB history: paper 1, paper 2, paper 3, and the historical investigation (internal assessment). The final chapter consists of exam-style questions. The chapters on papers 1, 2, and 3 go into detail on the types of questions that will be asked in these exams and how to go about answering them effectively. To help you see how to answer the questions, we have included authentic student samples from past exam sessions, complete with examiner comments. Each chapter will also discuss the markbands used by examiners and how you can use these to your advantage when answering exam questions. The chapter on the historical investigation will guide you through choosing a topic, developing a research question, conducting research, and putting the "identification and evaluation of sources", the "investigation", and the "reflection" all together in the final draft.

Key features of the book

Concept link

Concept links connect the contents of the chapter to the key concepts in the syllabus: causation, consequence, continuity, change, significance and perspectives.

QUESTION PRACTICE

An **exam paper icon** indicates that the question has been taken from a past IB paper.

↻ Reflection

Reflections are there to help you look critically at your own practices and how to improve them.

⟫ Assessment tip

Assessment tips are pieces of advice to help you optimize either your preparation for the exam or your time in the exam room while you are taking the exam. They will also warn you of common errors.

Question practice and sample student answers. These highlight the skills and content for each chapter. The annotations for each of these authentic student samples feature aspects of the questions that were positive and those which did not help the student to receive marks.

It is important to understand that, when examiners mark student responses, they are looking to award marks rather than deduct marks.

An example of a question practice section and an accompanying student answer is shown below.

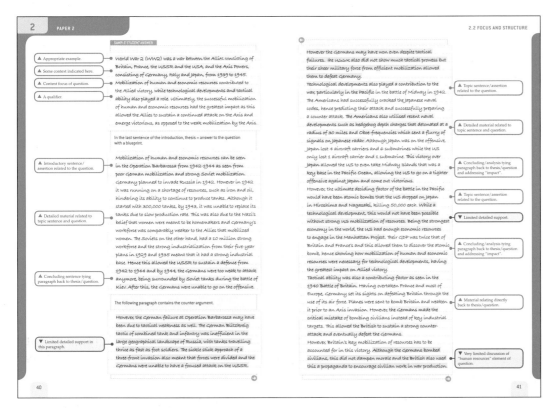

In both standard level and higher level history, there are a wide variety of options for study. You will study one of five prescribed subjects, two of twelve world history topics, and one of four regional options. The combinations and permutations of study options do not stop there. If you are studying the higher level course, your school will choose three sections within one of those four regional options. It is not feasible to cover all these subjects, topics, options, and sections in one book. Because of this, we have tried to choose as many representative samples as possible from the most common choices. Regardless of which choices your school has made, however, the skills, guidance, and advice in each chapter will be useful for any IB history student.

Exam strategies

Regardless of which options you are studying or which assessment component you are preparing for, there are some general strategies and guidelines that will help your success.

Manage your time. Use the mark weighting of the question to guide the relative amount of time to spend on each question. Avoid spending too much time on questions with which you are more comfortable. Use the clock in the exam room and listen to the announcements from the exam invigilator to guide your timing.

Understand the demands of the curriculum. When you are preparing for the exam, be sure to cover all required aspects of the curriculum. This means all the bulleted points in both case studies of the prescribed subject, all the prescribed content of the world history topics, and all the bulleted points of the three sections of your regional option if you are studying history at the higher level. Leave nothing out.

Read the question carefully. Be sure to answer the question that is asked and not the question you want to answer. The command terms are very important to this. If the question asks you to *analyse*, do not *describe*. You need to avoid overly narrative answers. Pay attention to terms such as *and*, *or*, and *both* in the question. There are no wasted words in an IB history exam question; they are all important. Does the question require examples from different regions? Does the question require a comparison, or can the examples be discussed independently? Does the question contain time parameters?

Be specific. Avoid general terminology and statements. Wherever possible, use precise names, dates, and terms. For example, if possible write "Strategic Arms Limitation Treaty" or "SALT I" rather than "a nuclear arms agreement".

Practise. When you are preparing, write a full-length response to at least one or two sample questions in the time limit set for the exam. This will give you an idea of how much you can write in the allotted time. Be sure to practise writing by hand if this is how you will be writing on exam day. Only use a word processor if you will be using one during the exam.

Stay focused on the question. Only use material and examples that are relevant to the question. You may have prepared for all aspects of a topic, say the Second World War, but if the question is asking about the causes of the Second World War, you should only use material related to the causes.

Stay the course. Once you have chosen the question, be very careful about changing your mind and starting another after the first 5–10 minutes. It is difficult to do a thorough job re-starting that far into the exam. You need to have a very sound and clear reason for changing questions.

Start strongly. In paper 2 and paper 3, answer the question you are most comfortable with first but stay focused on the time limit for the question.

Do	Don't
• Use the five minutes of reading time to organize your thoughts.	• Drop the names of historians into your response without a direct and detailed connection to the question being asked.
• Take a few minutes to plan your response on scrap paper.	• Write a pre-planned or "canned" response. For example, do not pre-plan an essay on the causes of the Cold War and use this regardless of the question being asked.
• Keep track of the time you have left.	
• Highlight, underline, and briefly annotate the exam paper to highlight important terms.	• Refer to people by their first names.
• Write legibly.	• Answer two questions from the same topic in paper 2.
• Clearly indicate which question you are answering.	• Make up historians. Examiners check on names they don't recognize.
• Write in blue or black ink.	• Answer questions on topics you have not studied in class, even if you think you know something about the topic.
• Review your responses before you hand your answers in, to quickly check for careless mistakes.	• Write a long, wordy introduction.
• Cross out material you do not want marked, such as planning.	• Include examples or evidence outside the time parameters of the question.
• Bring your response back to the thesis/question in a brief conclusion.	• Spend more than 2–4 minutes planning.

A note on balance and wellness

Balance and wellness are important components of the IB learner profile, and this applies to exam preparation as well. Even for strong students who are well prepared, exam sessions are stressful experiences. This means it is particularly important to take care of your physical and mental health while you prepare for exams.

• Eat properly and regularly during the exam period. Preparing for and writing exams is physically taxing, and your body requires fuel to continue to do it over the exam session.

• Get sufficient sleep during the exam period. Establishing a routine for sleep helps maximize the benefits of a good night's sleep. "All-nighters" are rarely worth the cost to your health and ability to concentrate. Get a good night's sleep the night before the exam.

• Avoid energy drinks and other artificial means for staying alert. Nothing is better than a balanced diet and regular sleep for helping you to stay alert.

• Stay active. Physical activity is important to a balanced life whether you are preparing for exams or not. At the very least, make sure you get outside as much as possible during this time.

• Take scheduled breaks. These allow you to maintain focus over a longer period. Plan activities, either relaxing or invigorating, for these breaks, as they will improve your concentration and give you something to look forward to.

• Maintain contact with your friends and classmates throughout the process. You are not alone in the process of preparing for these exams and you can provide support for one another.

• Give yourself plenty of time. Some exam stress can be alleviated by setting aside sufficient time to prepare for the exams, and starting to prepare well ahead of exams can alleviate anxiety and stress.

1 PAPER 1

You should be able to show:

- ✔ the structure of paper 1;
- ✔ understanding of historic sources;
- ✔ analysis and interpretation of a variety of sources;
- ✔ how to compare and contrast two sources;
- ✔ how to combine understanding of sources with your own knowledge to answer a historical question.

1.1   PAPER 1 OVERVIEW

Now that we have discussed what assessment looks like for IB history we are going to examine each paper more closely. Paper 1 is designed to test your use of the skills of a historian by asking you questions based on four brief sources relating to one of the case studies of your prescribed subject. The sources can take several forms. They can be from a range of written sources – books, periodicals, diaries, or speeches. They can be editorial cartoons or photographs, maps, graphs, or charts.

The structure of paper 1

The questions will always take the same pattern:

- First question: A two-part question asking for understanding of terms, ideas or content in the sources.

- Second question: A question asking you to analyse the value and limitations of one of the sources according to its origin, purpose, content.

- Third question: A question asking you to compare and contrast elements of two of the sources and what this reveals about a particular issue.

- Fourth question: A question asking you to evaluate a position given in the question based on the sources and your own knowledge of the case study of the prescribed subject.

The order of the questions reflects the steps that historians move through when investigating historical events using sources. Historians must first ensure that they understand what the source shows or demonstrates (first question). Once they understand the concepts, terms, and ideas in the source, historians must analyse the source to determine its value to the investigation as well as potential limitations (second question). Next, the source must be compared to other sources on the event. Do they agree? Where are the similarities? On what points do they contradict each other (third question)? Once this is complete, historians combine the information from the sources with what they already know about the topic under investigation to develop new understanding of the event (fourth question).

> **You should be able to:**
>
> - ✔ demonstrate an understanding of the structure of paper 1, including common types of questions and sources.

> **>> Assessment tip**
>
> The terms *primary source* and *secondary source* are descriptive; they have nothing to do with value and limitations. The fact that a source is a primary source does not necessarily make it more or less valuable than a secondary source and therefore does not need to form a part of your answer to the third question on paper 1.

We've already discussed how command terms are essential for understanding how a question should be answered. Likewise, not all questions are of equal difficulty. Some questions are more complex than others. Understanding various levels of questions and how they relate to each other can help you construct a strong answer to the question.

Benjamin Bloom was an educational psychologist who with his colleagues developed a way of classifying different levels of learning objectives to help teachers create better questions. The taxonomy is organized from more basic objectives / questions at the bottom to more complex intellectual activities at the top. Understanding his taxonomy can help you provide better answers to those questions.

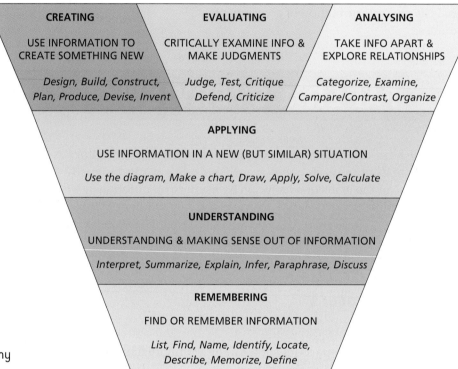

▶ Figure 1.1.1 Bloom's taxonomy diagram

QUESTION PRACTICE

Look at the following sample paper 1 questions, taken from the May 2017 exam paper. Classify each according to Bloom's taxonomy. What do you notice?

1 a) How, according to Source Q, were Albanians portrayed by Serbian propaganda? [3]

    b) What does Source R suggest about the perceptions some Serbian high school students had of Albanians in 1986? [2]

2 With reference to its origin, purpose, and content, analyse the value and limitations of Source S for an historian studying the rise of ethnic tensions between Serbs and Kosovar Albanians during the 1990s. [4]

3 Compare and contrast what Sources S and T reveal about the relations between Albanians and Serbs in Kosovo. [6]

4 Using the sources and your own knowledge, examine the reasons for the rise of ethnic nationalism in Kosovo during the early 1990s. [9]

Answers

1 Understanding

2 Analyse/Evaluate

3 Analyse

4 Create/Evaluate

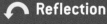 **Reflection**

Which questions seem more difficult? Why is that? How might this affect how you prepare for this exam?

The questions proceed from simple to complex. The mark value increases with the level of complexity of the question.

Based on the sources below, create four questions in the style of the paper 1 sample above. Be sure to use IB command terms when you construct your questions.

Source A

Earl Warren, US Chief Justice, delivers the decision of the US Supreme Court in Brown v Board of Education, 17 May 1954. Note: In the source, the word *Negro* is used to reflect the place and time of the original English language source. Today, in many countries, the word is no longer in common usage.

> We cannot turn the clock back to 1896 when Plessy versus Ferguson [a court judgment that had ruled that it was legal to have segregated schools as long as those schools had equal facilities] was written. We must consider public education in the full light of its present place in American life throughout the nation … In these days, it is doubtful that any child may reasonably be expected to succeed in life if he is denied the opportunity of an education … Such an opportunity, where the state has undertaken to provide it, is a right which must be available to all on equal terms.
>
> We come then to the question presented: Does segregation of children in schools on the basis of race, even though the facilities may be equal, deprive the children of the minority group of equal educational opportunities? We believe that it does … To separate Negro students from others solely because of their race generates a feeling of inferiority … that may affect their hearts and minds in a way unlikely ever to be undone …
>
> We conclude that in the field of public education the doctrine of "separate but equal" has no place. Separate educational facilities are unequal.

Source B

Photograph of protesters at a pro-segregation rally in Baltimore, 1954. The posters at the front of the photograph read: "We want our rights"; "We can't fight alone. Join us now!"; "We can't fight alone".

Source C

Tom Brady, a judge and a leader of the pro-segregation White Citizens' Council movement, writing about his speech to the Indianola Citizens' Council in his pamphlet "A Review of Black Monday" (28 October 1954).

The Supreme Court says, "You have got to sit a black boy down by a white girl to have it equal." …

You can't do it! You can't put little boys and little girls together—blacks and whites and have them sing together, play together, dance together, and eat together, sit side by side, and walk arm in arm, and expect for the sensitivity of those white children not to be broken down. You can't do it! Why? That is exactly what has happened in the north, [but] they have a sufficient number of whites to absorb, and perhaps assimilate, the blacks …

We can see what happens on the surface. We don't know what happens to the brain of [a black] man … We don't know what it takes to make his mind different from our mind.

This Supreme Court sets aside all the laws of biology! By putting these children together in schools we will abolish all racial differences that God made. I have a little field [at the] back of my home. I notice the blackbirds stay together … I notice the geese and the ducks stayed separate from each other and yet the Supreme Court would set aside these basic laws of God and of nature and compel these various individuals to mingle, just as you would blackbirds with partridges …

Source D

Michael Klarman, a professor of history, writing about the effect of the Supreme Court's 1955 judgment, Brown II, in the academic book *Brown v Board of Education and the Civil Rights Movement* (2007). In Brown II, the Supreme Court decided on "gradualism", that is, the gradual application of the Supreme Court's decision in Brown v Board of Education (1954) to end school segregation.

Brown II was a clear victory for white southerners … The Court approved gradualism, imposed no deadlines for beginning or completing desegregation, issued vague guidelines, and entrusted the final decision to local judges. When informed of the decision, Florida legislators [law-makers] broke into cheers … A Mississippi politician celebrated the fact that a local Mississippi judge would decide when desegregation would be feasible [practical]. Southern law-makers commented that desegregation might be feasible in another fifty or one hundred years.

Black leaders were disappointed with the decision … A black journalist, John H. McCray, admitted that he "can't find too much to cheer about", and he criticized the Supreme Court for "seeking to do business" with diehard [determined] southern segregationists.

>> **Assessment tip**

The total time allowed for paper 1 is 60 minutes (although you will get 5 additional minutes of reading time at the beginning during which you are not allowed to write anything). You should use the mark value for each question to determine roughly how many minutes to allocate to answer each question. The total mark value for paper 1 is 24 marks. If we divide this by the 60 minutes you have to complete the paper, we get about 2.5 minutes per mark. Applying this to the questions we get the following:

Question	Approximate time allocation
First a) and b)	12.5 minutes
Second	10 minutes
Third	15 minutes
Fourth	22.5 minutes

Remember, this is an approximation and is intended as a guide only. It is designed to help you stay on track while writing the paper.

The following terms are used in paper 1 so it is important to understand their meaning. How to address these terms in the context of the paper 1 questions will be covered in the following sections.

>> **Assessment tip**

Complete the questions in order. The thinking required for the early questions will help you answer the final question.

- **Origin** – When referring to a source, the origin is when, where, and by whom was the source created.

- **Purpose** – This describes the reason that the source was created. Was it designed to persuade somebody? Was it designed to be an honest account? Was it created to justify a position? Understanding the intended audience for a source can help you determine its purpose.

- **Content** – Simply put, the content of a source is a description of what it says or depicts. In the context of the second question on paper 1, you will need to discuss how this content helps or does not help the historian understand the specific issue. Simply describing the content will receive no marks.

- **Value** – In terms of paper 1, the value of a source refers to why the source is important or useful to a historian studying the subject of the source.

- **Limitations** – When determining the limitations of a source you are looking for factors in or about the source that would hinder the historian from getting a complete view of the event being studied.

- **Compare and contrast** – To give an account of similarities and differences between two (or more) items or situations, referring to both (all) of them throughout.

- **With reference to ...** – Making a direct/explicit link in your answer to the components listed in the question. For example, in the second question of paper 1, linking your response directly to the origin, purpose, and content of the source.

- **Examine** – To consider an argument or concept in a way that uncovers the assumptions and interrelationships of the issue.

- **Discuss** – To offer a considered and balanced review that includes a range of arguments, factors, or hypotheses. Opinions or conclusions should be presented clearly and supported by appropriate evidence.

- **Analyse** – To break down in order to bring out the essential elements or structure, and explain how these elements relate to each other.

- **To what extent …** – To consider the merits or otherwise of an argument or a concept. This requires you to consider positions on both sides of an argument. Opinions and conclusions should be presented clearly and supported with appropriate evidence and sound argument.

1.2   THE FIRST QUESTION

You should be able to:

✔ demonstrate understanding of a source;

✔ interpret a source.

Understanding and interpreting a source

The first question in paper 1 requires you to demonstrate the most basic skill of a historian … understanding what a source is saying or depicting. This can range from a basic understanding of certain terms or phrases in the document to an interpretation of the meaning of a document. While the direct meaning of terms can be straightforward, some questions will require you to determine what the source implies about an issue. In these cases it will be necessary to look at the deeper meaning of the source.

The first question is divided into two parts, a) and b). Generally part a) will ask you the literal or direct meaning of parts of a document – more of a denotation question. Part b), on the other hand, will generally ask what a source *suggests* about a topic.

For example:

> **a)** What, according to Source M, was the Italian motivation for the invasion of Abyssinia? [3]
>
> **b)** What does Source O suggest about the impact of the Hoare–Laval Pact on the Abyssinian Crisis? [2]

Notice that part a) is asking what the direct meaning of Source M reveals about Italian motivation for the invasion. There is no need to go beyond what is written in the source. Part b), however, wants you to demonstrate an understanding of something that the source *suggests* that does go beyond what is explicitly depicted in the source. It requires you to make a connection between what is in the source and a historical issue that is not directly mentioned in the source, which is a more complex task. In this example, the source would not directly state what the impact of the Hoare–Laval Pact had on the Abyssinian Crisis.

» Assessment tip

Part a) is worth three marks and part b) is worth two marks. This means that you should have at least three distinct points for part a) and at least two distinct points for part b).

Reading for understanding

The first question in paper 1 is testing your understanding of the sources. Practising and using reading comprehension strategies can help you better understand the sources and therefore get a better mark on this part of the assessment. Here are some techniques that will help you better understand what you are reading. You need to be an active reader. Having said that, it is important to keep your eye on the clock. You should only take about 12 minutes to answer the above question so you will not likely be able to do all of these in the exam room, but they will help you develop the skills necessary for paper 1.

Highlight/Underline – When you read a source, underline or highlight important phrases, people, events, dates, and historic terms. This will do two things. It will make it easier to find these when you are writing your answers. More broadly, it will help you retrieve information you have studied by triggering your memory. Be sure to highlight/ underline the important information in the contextual material for all the sources as well. As this strategy does not take much more time than simply reading, you should be able to use this one in the exam room.

Annotate – As you move through the source, write down information that comes to mind that is not in the source. Write this information on the source booklet itself or on a separate piece of paper. For example, if the source mentions Woodrow Wilson, you might jot down "US President, Treaty of Versailles" in the margin. This will help you start organizing information in your head and help you answer the part b) question as that is the part of the question that asks you to make connections with information not explicitly in the source.

Restate – Restating or writing complex sentences in your own words can help you understand their meaning and save you from having to re-read it several times as you move back and forth between the sources, the questions, and your answers. Be sure not to take up too much time doing this, however. Save this strategy for the trickiest passages.

Question – Questioning is an important component of understanding. As you move through the sources, jot down any questions that come to mind. This will prove useful when you are answering the second, third, and fourth questions. For example, simply writing down *Why?* or *What did this lead to?* beside a passage can help you analyse the limitations of the source for the second question.

Reflection

Choose a source that you have studied this year or use Source G (page 9). As you read it, practise the strategies above and answer the following reflection questions:

1 How much more time did it take to actively read the sources than to skim them?

2 Which of the four strategies listed above did you find the most useful? Why do you think that is the case?

Source E

An extract from a Japanese government statement, "The Fundamental Principles of National Policy" (August 1936).

(1) Japan must strive to eradicate [eliminate] the aggressive policies of the great powers …

(3) … in order to promote Manchukuo's healthy development and to stabilize Japan–Manchukuo national defense, the threat from the north, the Soviet Union, must be eliminated; in order to promote our economic development, we must prepare against Great Britain and the United States and bring about close collaboration between Japan, Manchukuo, and China. In the execution of this policy, Japan must pay due attention to friendly relations with other powers.

(4) Japan plans to promote her racial and economic development in the South Seas, especially in the outlying South Seas area. She plans to extend her strength by moderate and peaceful means without arousing other powers. In this way, concurrently with the firm establishment of Manchukuo, Japan must expect full development and strengthening of her national power.

Source F

William Beasley, a professor of the history of the Far East, writing in the academic book *Japanese Imperialism, 1894–1945* (1987).

Central to the basic propositions was the intention that Japan … must establish cordial [friendly] relations with the peoples of the area founded on the principles of co-existence and co-prosperity. It would also undertake economic expansion on its own account by creating a strong coalition between Japan, Manchukuo, and China and by extending its interests in South-East Asia in gradual and peaceful ways. There were some conditions. The army must be given forces in Korea and Kwantung [Guandong] sufficient to deal with any attack from Soviet Russia. The navy must have a fleet capable of maintaining ascendancy in the west Pacific against that of the United States.

Sino-Japanese [Chinese–Japanese] cooperation, designed to detach Nanking [Nanjing] from its communist affiliations [links], though highly desirable must not be allowed to stand in the way of treating north China as a "special region" to be brought into close relationship with Japan and Manchukuo.

It was, for example, to provide strategic materials, in order to strengthen their defences against the Soviet Union. As to the south, a gradual and peaceful approach was intended to avert fears in countries of the area concerning Japanese aims …

From the point of view of the ministers in Tokyo, none of this was meant to bring about territorial expansion. They still thought in terms of informal empire, that is, of securing an increase in Japan's privileges through pressure exerted on Asian governments, including that of China.

Source G

Hans van de Ven, a professor of modern Chinese history, writing in the academic book *War and Nationalism in China: 1925–1945* (2003).

By 1933, Japan's military strategy aimed at defending itself against the Soviet Union, China and the British and American navies. Massive investment programmes in the heavy, chemical, and machinery industries followed to give Japan the industrial base to sustain itself in time of war, and also of course to deal with the problems of the Depression. In 1936, Japan stepped up its military expenditures when a new cabinet accepted the build-up of national strength as Japan's highest priority …

Japan therefore developed a strategic doctrine aimed at defending Japan by aggressive offensive operations of limited duration, to be concluded before its major enemies could concentrate their forces in East Asia. To defeat China before such a war was part of this strategy. Worried about war with the Soviet Union and the Western powers, the "removal of China", as the aggressive General Tojo stated in a telegram from Manchuria to Tokyo in early 1937, would eliminate "an important menace from our rear" and release forces for service on more critical fronts. If the military build-up and the political influence of the army in Japanese politics were causes for worry in China, so were the expansionist tendencies of the Kwantung [Guandong] Army in Manchuria.

Source H

John Bernard Partridge, an illustrator and cartoonist, depicts Japan threatening China in an untitled cartoon for the British magazine *Punch* (21 July 1937). Note: The word on the tail is Manchukuo.

S.O.S.

Chinese dragon: I say, do be careful with that sword! If you try to cut off my head I shall really have to appeal to the League again.

Question

a) What, according to Source E, were the challenges facing Japanese national policy? [3]

b) What does Source H suggest about Sino-Japanese [Chinese–Japanese] relations in 1937? [2]

Part a) asks for challenges facing Japanese foreign policy and it is worth three marks. That means you should have three distinct "challenges". There is no need to go beyond what is in the source.

▲ This is a valid challenge taken directly from clause (3) of the source.

▲ This is a valid challenge taken directly from clause (3) of the source.

▲ This is a valid challenge taken directly from clause (4) of the source.

a) According to source E, the first challenge that faced Japanese national policy is to eliminate the Soviet Union in order to promote Manchukuo's development and stabilized defence. The second challenge is to prepare against Great Britain and the United States in order to promote economic development in Manchukuo. The last challenge is to extend its strength peacefully, and without stimulating other powers.

This response could have achieved 3/3 marks.

Part b) asks for what the source suggests about "Sino-Japanese [Chinese–Japanese] relations" and is worth two marks. This means you should have two distinct points.

▲ Valid suggestions from the source, they show an understanding of the message that the cartoon is trying to give about Sino-Japanese relations.

b) Source H suggests that Japan was in a superior position than China. This is shown from how the samurai is grabbing the Chinese dragon's neck, and holding up a sword. It also suggests that Manchukuo was forcibly taken away and was not dealt peacefully. This is shown from the Chinese dragon's dialogue.

The answer to part b) explains briefly where the suggestions come from in the source. This is not strictly necessary given the command terms of the question, but is fine. The answer could also legitimately state that Chinese–Japanese relations were strained.

This response could have achieved 2/2 marks.

1.3   THE SECOND QUESTION

You should be able to:

✔ determine the origin, purpose, and content of a historical source;

✔ understand how origin, purpose, and content affect the value and limitations of a source.

Why are these sources useful?

While the first question in paper 1 generally deals with knowledge and understanding, the second question focuses more on analysis and evaluation, and, as such, is more complex. As mentioned earlier, it is the next step that a historian takes when faced with a question to investigate and a number of sources to use. Once you understand what the source is saying, you must determine what it can tell you and what its limitations are.

Before we can determine how useful a source is, we must first consider certain pieces of information about the source that will help us evaluate the value and limitations. For the purposes of the second question on paper 1 these factors are *origin*, *purpose*, and *content*.

> • **Origin** – The origin of a source is the answer to three *Ws*. Who created the source? When was the source created? Where was the source created?
>
> • **Purpose** – This is the *why* of the source. Why was it created? What was the intended audience?
>
> • **Content** – What does the source say regarding a specific historic event/issue?

Determining the origin of a source

Often, the material needed to establish the origin of a source in paper 1 is given in the contextual information at the beginning of the source. The following is taken from a source for prescribed subject 4.

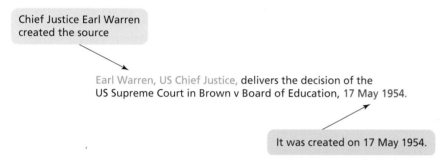

▲ Figure 1.3.1 Determining the origin of a source

Notice in the above sample there is no place indicated. We can assume the source comes from Washington, DC, as that is where the United States Supreme Court is located. This may or may not be significant to the value and limitations of the source.

Determining the purpose of the source

To help us establish why a source was created, we can look at two aspects of the document – the type of document and the intended audience of the document. The first aspect is the type of document. Certain generic types of documents are created for specific purposes and this can be used to help answer the second question. For example, a newspaper editorial's purpose is to express the opinion of the writer on a subject. On the other hand, an article in a newspaper is designed to communicate the *facts* of a story as understood at the time. The same applies to secondary sources. History textbooks are generally written to educate the audience. Understanding why a source was created will help us determine the *value* and *limitation* component of this question. The following chart is a starting point.

▼ **Table 1.3.1** Different types of sources

Type of source	Description	Purpose	Possible effect on value of source	Possible effect on limitations of source
Memoirs	Compiled recollections often written long after the events depicted.	To express the author's perception of the events and his or her role in them. Generally, for public consumption.	They can give first-hand accounts of people who were at the event and their perspective on the event.	They are often written long after the events and can therefore be subject to questionable recollections. They can be written to justify actions.
Diaries	Personal thoughts or reflections on subjects or events – often recorded at the time of the event.	To help the author better understand events and themselves. Perhaps record things for future personal remembrance.	Because they are seldom intended for any audience other than the author, diaries can be candid impressions of the writer.	As they are generally very personal impressions, diaries might not consider other perspectives on the issue. They could be written in the understanding that they may be public in the future.
Letters	Private correspondence between individuals. Not generally intended for public consumption.	To explain personal motivations, thoughts, opinions to another individual.	Personal letters that are not intended for the public to read can express candid and honest impressions or motivations.	They are generally from a single perspective. They do not indicate the response from the person receiving the letter, which would make them more valuable.
Legislation	Laws enacted by a government.	Indicates government intentions and what it expects of its citizens.	Laws indicate the official goals and intentions of a government.	The legislation itself does not indicate the reaction to the law or the degree to which it was supported in the legislature. Who supported it? Who opposed it? Does not often explain motivations for the law. Was the law enacted or enforced?
Speeches	Public statements by significant figures.	To inform or convince the audience of the speaker's intentions, ideas, policies, etc.	Speeches indicate what the speaker wanted the audience to know. They often indicate the arguments in favour of a position.	What was the response to the speech? How large was the audience? What has the speaker left out in order to convince the audience?
Editorials and editorial cartoons	Opinions in published news sources. Cartoons express the opinion through satire.	To communicate the writer's or publication's opinion on a topic or an issue.	Editorials indicate the position of the publication on the issue. Depending on the circulation of the publication, editorials can give some indication of the public's position on an issue.	Editorials do not often include the counter arguments to the position. Does it reflect public opinion or is it seeking to influence public opinion?
Maps	Graphic depictions of geographical bodies.	To aid navigation and illustrate knowledge about a geographical area.	Maps can indicate how the creator and his or her society view the world. For example, world maps that place Europe at the centre may indicate a Eurocentric view of the world.	They can be from limited perspectives. There might be little context for the data in the map.
Academic histories	Investigations based on source analysis published by professional historians.	To explore and communicate cause, consequence, change, continuity, perspective, and significance of historical events and people.	They can offer an interpretation that is balanced between different viewpoints. They are generally created by consulting multiple sources. They have the benefit of "historical distance".	They can be limited by the information available at the time it was created. They can be written from an ideological perspective.
Memos and other government documents	Official communications within a government.	To communicate between government officials or departments – not generally for public consumption.	Because they are not generally intended to be read by the public, these documents can provide candid opinions, intentions, and motivations of governments.	Memos will often be limited to the perspective of the government in question and not provide an indication of how well supported the position might be.

Why is it important to know the intended audience of a source?

In the same way that you adjust the way you write based on who will be reading it – for example, a text message to a friend has a very different style and tone from an essay written for your history teacher – historical sources are often dependent on the intended audience and this affects the purpose of the source. A speech written for a graduation and directed at students would have a different purpose than one delivered in parliament or congress for politicians.

A word about content

Content is the third aspect of the source that we will use to help determine the value and limitations of the source. It is important to relate the content to the given issue, as it helps you avoid simply paraphrasing the source and therefore lifts it above a simple *remember* response. What does the content tell us about the issue and what does it leave out?

How do we establish the value and limitations of a source?

The second question on paper 1 asks you to use the origin, purpose, and content to determine the value and limitations of the source in investigating a given issue related to the sources. The given issue is important because it gives you a focus for your answer. The question is not asking for the general value and limitations of the source, so your answer must be connected to the issue.

Consider the following question taken from the May 2017 exam, for prescribed subject 5:

> With reference to its origin, purpose and content, analyse the value and limitations of Source S for an historian studying the rise of ethnic tensions between Serbs and Kosovar Albanians during the 1990s. [4]

In this case, we must focus on how the source sheds light on ethnic tensions between Serbs and Kosovar Albanians. We can use this to make the generic description in Table 1.3.1 more specific to the question. If Source S was, for example, a Serbian government memo, it would be valuable in that it would tell a historian what the Serbian government candidly thought about its relationship with the Kosovar Albanians because government memos are not generally intended for release to the public. On the other hand, if Source S had been a speech by a Serbian government official, part of the value would be that the source would tell the historian what the Serbian government wanted the audience to think its attitude to the tension was. Source S was in fact from Djuric Bosko, a Serb who moved out of Kosovo, being interviewed by an American researcher in 1995.

The origin can make the source valuable for a variety of reasons. Sources created at the time of the issue or event being studied can indicate a contemporary understanding or an eyewitness account. The farther the date of the document is from the event being studied, the more this value is lost. Eyewitness reports written down long after the event can be affected by the inaccuracy of memory and so can also be a limitation. On the other hand, a source created long after the event can have the advantage of historic distance, allowing for the account to be more reasoned.

A note on *bias*

The word *bias* means a prejudice in favour or opposed to one perspective and as such can be applied to almost any sources in one way or another. By itself, bias does not tell us that much about the value or limitations of the source. For example, a speech by President Franklin Roosevelt would certainly be biased toward his policies, but this alone is not a comment on the value or limitations of the source. What is perhaps more important is to explain how this potential bias, combined with the content of the source, relates to the issue highlighted in the second question.

Structuring your answer

The second question is asking you to examine how the origin, purpose, and content of the source affect its value and limitation for a historian studying a historical issue. It therefore makes sense to structure your response into two paragraphs. One should examine how origin, purpose, and content would help a historian studying the issue – the value. The second paragraph should do the same for the limitations of the source.

>> **Assessment tip**

Do not use the fact that the source may be a translation or an excerpt as either a strength or a weakness. You are NOT being asked to explain how the form (excerpt/translation) impacts the value and limitations.

QUESTION PRACTICE

Source I

Daniel Patrick Moynihan, a former US Navy officer and a sociologist who was Assistant Secretary of Labor for President Lyndon B. Johnson, writing in the report *The Negro Family: The Case for National Action* (March 1965).

Delinquency and crime

The combined impact of poverty, failure, and isolation among Negro youth has had the predictable outcome in a disastrous delinquency and crime rate … It is probable that, at present, a majority of the crimes against the person are committed by Negroes. There is, of course, no absolute evidence; inference can only be made from arrest and prison population statistics … In Chicago in 1963, three-quarters of the persons arrested for such crimes were Negro; in Detroit, the proportions were the same. In 1960, 37% of all persons in Federal and State prisons were Negro. In that year, 56% of the homicide and 57% of the assault offenders committed to State institutions were Negro …

The Armed Forces

The ultimate mark of inadequate preparation for life is the failure rate on the Armed Forces mental test … A grown young man who cannot pass this test is in trouble. 56% of Negroes fail it. This is a rate almost four times that of the whites … Service in the United States Armed Forces is the only experience open to the Negro American in which he is truly treated as an equal … In food, dress, housing, pay, work—the Negro in the Armed Forces is equal and is treated that way.

Question

With reference to its origin, purpose, and content, analyse the value and limitations of Source I for a historian studying the social position of African Americans in the US.   [4]

This source is an excerpt of the report 'The Negro Family: The Case for National Action' written by Daniel Patrick Moynihan and released in March 1965. The purpose of this source is to outline the position of presumably different members of an African American (Negro) family within American society. It is therefore useful to a historian studying the social position of African Americans as it gives an account of the sociology of African Americans' point of view from an expert point of view seeing as the author is a sociologist. Furthermore, the content of the source is backed up using numerical data, adding to the credibility of the source, proving it useful for historians. However, this source is limited as it speaks about 'the Negro family' within the context of them being in need of 'National Action'. This then makes the source one-sided towards the faults of African Americans within American society. This is then limited to the historian in question as it only shows the negative social position of African Americans, rather than their social position as a whole.

▲ The origin and purpose of the document are laid out clearly. Note, all this information is taken directly from the contextual material at the beginning of the source.

▲ This is the focus of the question.

▲ The value the source is directly related to the origin, by noting it is from the point of view of an expert.

▲ The value of the content of the source is effectively explained here.

▲ This portion of the response indicates how the purpose, as outlined in the title of the source, is a limitation.

▲ Note that the response explains why the purpose is a limitation, rather than simply stating it is a limitation.

This response effectively analyses the value associated with the origin of the document, the value associated with the content of the document, and a limitation associated with the purpose. It therefore deals with all the components of the question.

This response could have achieved 4/4 marks.

Reflection

What are the strengths of the above response? What would you add to improve it?

1.4 THE THIRD QUESTION

You should be able to:

✔ compare and contrast two sources relative to a historical question or issue.

The next step: How do the sources compare to each other?

Once a historian has determined how valuable a source could be and what the potential limitations of that source are, the next step is to see how the content of the source compares to what other sources say about the topic under investigation. You must pull the sources apart and determine the similarities and differences between these elements.

It is important to understand that, to do well on this question, you must do more than simply list the similarities and the differences. Nor should you merely describe the sources as this leaves the comparing up to the reader. You must integrate both sources into a running discussion of the similarities and differences.

The most straightforward integrated structure is to use one paragraph to examine how the two documents are similar and then a second paragraph to examine the differences in the sources. Just make sure you integrate elements of both sources in each paragraph.

QUESTION PRACTICE

1 Compare and contrast what Sources I and J (from exam paper May 2017) reveal about the increasing tensions between the US and Japan. (Note these two sources I and J are not reproduced in this book.) [6]

2 Compare and contrast what Sources F and G (pages 8-9) reveal about Japanese foreign policy aims in East Asia. [6]

SAMPLE STUDENT ANSWER

▼ This is a simple description of Source I.

▼ Likewise, this is a description of Source J.

1) According to source I, the tensions between the US and Japan began when Japan moved to Indochina and the US expanded the export embargo. This provoked the Japanese military to strike against the US and its allies. Source J says that yes war was inevitable, but the tensions rose because of the oil supply. Both sources state that the US (Roosevelt) cutting off all oil supply to Japan caused tensions.

This response is a description of the two sources with no attempt to integrate the content of the sources to answer the question; therefore it rests in the 1–2 markband.

This response could have achieved 2/6 marks.

▼ There are three valid points of comparison in this paragraph, but they lack clarity and detail.

▼ While there is more detail in this portion of the response, it is very descriptive.

2) Source F and G both discuss about Japan's imperialism and its expansion and invasion of Manchuria. They both mention that Japan was interested in economic and military expansion, so as to defend itself from the west, especially the United States and the Soviet Union. Both reasoned that Japan felt that China was in their sole interest as part of their military strategy of defence. However source F portrays the invasion of the Japanese in Manchukuo as more peaceful and gradual. It emphasizes that Japan was not interested in territorial expansion but rather peaceful co-existence and securing Japan's defence. It portrays that this peaceful approach was taken so as to divert attention from the central European powers away from its expansion and it really desired close relations with China.

▲ Some limited attempt to integrate the sources.

▼ The rest of this part of the response is quite descriptive.

Source G contradicts this as it suggests that Japan was aggressive in their strategy, using diction such as 'removal of China'. It portrays that the Japanese did not only invade Manchuria for the purpose of defence but also had underlying expansionist tendencies toward Manchuria to build up national strength in Asia.

This response could have achieved 4/6 marks.

There is another way to structure your response to the third question. You should look for elements common to both sources you are examining and then compare and contrast the sources across these elements. Potential elements to compare will generally be particular to the two sources, but often you can use one or more of the following historical concepts:

- Change
- Continuity
- Causation
- Consequence
- Perspective
- Significance.

For example, you can explain the similarities and differences in how two sources approach the cause of an event.

Within these causes, you might be able to explore aspects such as economics, politics, or social elements. Two sources discussing the causes of the First World War, for example, could be broken down into economic and political causes and then compared.

In terms of structuring your response, using this method means you would use a paragraph for each of themes that you discuss. For example, one paragraph exploring the similarities and differences in how each source relates to the political causes of a war and another explaining how each source relates to the economic causes of the war could be an effective way of answering this question.

You can use several ways to analyse the source to determine the similarities and differences. If you are going to structure your response as one paragraph for similarities and one paragraph for differences, then you could use some form of a Venn diagram to determine these similarities and differences.

QUESTION PRACTICE

Source J

Peter Jackson, a professor of medieval history, writing in an academic book, *The Mongols and the West, 1221–1410* (2005).

The cohesiveness of the Mongol military stood in sharp contrast with the disunity of their enemies, which Genghis Khan and his successors took care to exploit. The political fragmentation of early 13th-century Rus' under the prolific Riurikid dynasty is well known. But division also characterized the two most formidable powers confronting the Mongols. Jurchen rule was deeply resented by the Khitan still living in the borderlands of China, large numbers of whom joined the Mongols or coordinated their own operations against the Chin [Jin] with those of Mongol commanders. Subsequently, even native Chinese and Jurchen officers and troops defected to the invaders. In western Asia, the Khwarazm shah's bitter quarrel with the 'Abbasid Caliph impaired [weakened] his capacity to pose as a champion of orthodoxy and the Jihad, while the unreliability of significant elements in his recently gained dominions undermined his preparations for resistance. By contrast, the religious tolerance that characterized Genghis Khan's empire also served the Mongols well, so that the Gur-khan's Muslim subjects in eastern Turkestan, who had been persecuted by Kuchlug, welcomed them as liberators.

Source K

Jack Weatherford, a professor of anthropology and a specialist in tribal peoples, writing in an academic book, *Genghis Khan and the Making of the Modern World* (2004).

[Mongol] tactics seemed to be, at least in part, an amalgamation [combination] of older fighting techniques and hunting strategies; yet the consistent inability of the perplexed [confused] enemy to respond effectively to this form of warfare indicated that Temujin [Genghis Khan] had introduced enough innovation to make these strategies uniquely his own. Temujin had produced a new type of steppe army based on a greater variety of tactics and, most important, close cooperation among the men and complete obedience to their commanders. They were no longer an attacking horde of individuals; they were now a united formation. Temujin used a set of manoeuvres that each man had to know and to which each responded precisely and without hesitation. The Mongols had a saying: "If he sends me into fire or water I go. I go for him." The saying reflected not just an ideal, but the reality of the new Mongol warfare, and it made short order of [rapidly defeated] the Naiman.

Question

Compare and contrast what Sources J and K reveal about the factors that led to the success of Genghis Khan's military campaigns and tactics. **[6]**

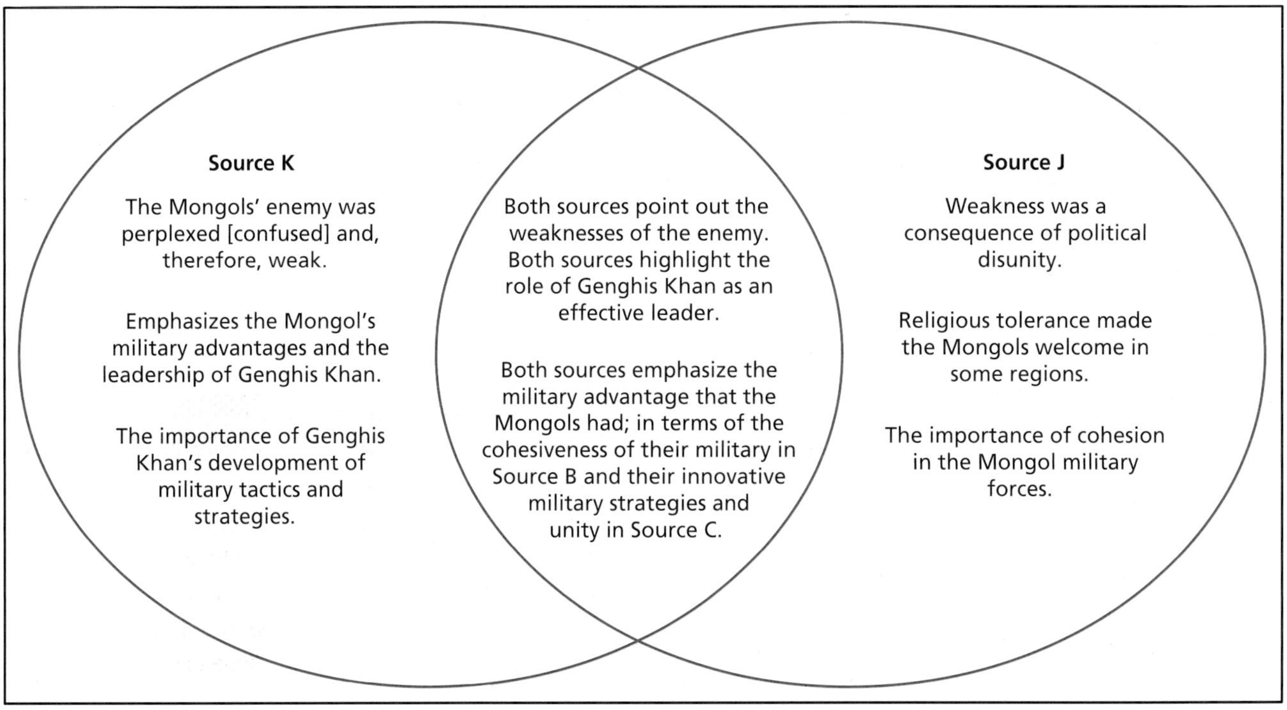

Source K

The Mongols' enemy was perplexed [confused] and, therefore, weak.

Emphasizes the Mongol's military advantages and the leadership of Genghis Khan.

The importance of Genghis Khan's development of military tactics and strategies.

Both sources point out the weaknesses of the enemy. Both sources highlight the role of Genghis Khan as an effective leader.

Both sources emphasize the military advantage that the Mongols had; in terms of the cohesiveness of their military in Source B and their innovative military strategies and unity in Source C.

Source J

Weakness was a consequence of political disunity.

Religious tolerance made the Mongols welcome in some regions.

The importance of cohesion in the Mongol military forces.

▲ Figure 1.4.1 Venn diagram determining similarities and differences of Sources J and K

If you are using the thematic approach, a straightforward chart might help you to organize your thoughts. In the above case you would create one paragraph based on the leadership theme and one paragraph based on the theme of the military, integrating material from both sources into each paragraph.

Theme	Source J	Source K
Leadership	• The Khwarazm shah was a weak leader • Weakness was a consequence of disunity • Enemies unable to organize effective resistance • Religious tolerance made the Mongols welcome in some regions	• Khan confused his enemies • Khan combined hunting and military tactics – innovation • Inspired loyalty in his troops • Emphasizes the leadership of Genghis Khan
Military	• Not unified, weak • Jurchen rule was deeply resented by the Khitan – defected to Khan • The Khwarazm shah had unreliable elements in his army	• Khan's army was unified • Khan's army well trained and loyal

> **>> Assessment tip**
>
> Regardless of which organizing strategy you use, be sure not to spend too much time on it. Remember, you have roughly 15 minutes to complete this question and that includes any planning you may do.

Evaluation and the third question: markbands

The third and fourth questions on paper 1 are marked according to two distinct sets of markbands. Markbands are a series of statements that describe different levels of achievement. Markers will compare your response to the descriptors and see which level the response most closely matches. It is therefore important for you to know what each of these levels of achievement look like.

These are the markbands for the third question on paper 1. A different set of markbands are used for the fourth question, paper 2, and paper 3.

Marks	Level descriptor
5–6	• The response includes clear and valid points of comparison **and** of contrast.
3–4	• The response includes some valid points of comparison and/or of contrast, although these points may lack clarity.
1–2	• The response consists of description of the content of the source(s), and/or general comments about the source(s), rather than valid points of comparison or of contrast.
0	• The response does not reach a standard described by the descriptors above.

Source: IB history specimen paper

> **⟳ Reflection**
>
> What do you think are the most important words in these markbands? Based on these markbands and in your own words, how would you describe a *good* response to this question?

There are several things to take note of in the markbands for this question. The first is that, if you simply describe what is in the sources, leaving the comparing and contrasting up to the reader, you cannot score more than 2 marks. The other dominant characteristic of responses that fall into this markband is that they are general rather than specific.

The 3–4 markband is characterized by the inclusion of some effort at explaining the similarities and/or the differences. If you neglect to examine *both* similarities and differences, 4 marks would be the most you could achieve on this question. If your response lacks clarity, it may also fall into this markband, so be sure to explain the similarities and differences in detail.

The top markband describes responses that examine *both* similarities and differences in detail. It is generally a good idea to have at least two valid points of comparison and at least two valid points of contrast with some comment.

1.5   THE FOURTH QUESTION

> **You should be able to:**
>
> ✔ use sources to answer a question on a historical issue;
>
> ✔ combine the source knowledge with your own knowledge to answer a historical question.

Putting it all together

The fourth question in paper 1 requires you to use the information you have gained from the sources and combine it with material you have studied to answer a question. In many ways, this is the culmination of the historian's work. Once he or she understands what a source is saying, the historian must then understand what the value and limitations of the source are, after which it must be compared to other sources. It is at this point that the historian uses the information from the sources with his or her own knowledge of history to create new historical knowledge.

This question is worth 9 marks. Therefore, your answer should generally be longer than the answers for the other three questions and take you about 22 minutes of the allotted 60 minutes to answer.

It is important to remember that the question being asked will relate to one of the bulleted points in one of the case studies in your prescribed subject. You must therefore prepare for all the bullet points in both case studies to be ready for this paper.

Structuring your response

Essentially, this question is asking you to write a mini-essay. There is not enough time to write an entire introduction, but the task does revolve around a central question with a command term and requires you to have a focused answer. One way to do this is to write a thesis statement – the answer to the question – without the rest of the introduction. For example, look at this question taken from the November 2017 exam for prescribed subject 1:

> Using the sources and your own knowledge, to what extent do you agree that Mongol military strength under Genghis Khan contributed to the Mongol takeover of Central Asia and the Near East?   [9]

A thesis for this question could be:

> "While military strength was the primary reason for the Mongol takeover of Central Asia and the Near East, religious policies also contributed to this takeover."

Note that the thesis above directly addresses the question while accounting for the command term *to what extent* by using the qualifier

> **>> Assessment tip**
>
> When you use information from one of the sources, identify that source in square brackets after the information. For example, [Source A].

or counter argument regarding "religious policies". The rest of the response must now be focused on this thesis statement.

Here's another example from the May 2017 exam for prescribed subject 3:

> "Mutual fear led to increasing tensions between the US and Japan." Using the sources and your own knowledge, to what extent do you agree with this statement? [9]

A thesis for this question could be:

> "While mutual fear did lead to increasing tensions between the United States and Japan, it was primarily the result of Japan's need for resources to fuel its expansion in China."

The most effective way to organize the rest of the response is to integrate both your own knowledge and information from the sources. It is far less effective to separate the information in the sources into one paragraph and your own knowledge into another. There is no set number of paragraphs for this task. A well-constructed paragraph should develop a central idea. It starts with a topic sentence that outlines the central idea, followed by two or three sentences with specific evidence relating to that idea. This specific evidence comes from the sources and the from the material that you have studied. The paragraph concludes with a sentence that links the previous sentences together and relates back to the question being asked.

Reflection

How could you improve on these two thesis statements?

Assessment tip

Take one or two minutes to sketch out a brief outline of what your response will look like.

Evaluation and the fourth question: more markbands

As with the third question on paper 1, markbands are also used to evaluate responses to the fourth question. They are, however, different markbands. The markbands for the third question focused on one dimension of the response – how well the response understood the similarities and differences in relation to the theme of the question. For the fourth question, the markbands describe levels of achievement across three elements:

- Focus
- Use of sources
- Own knowledge.

Marks	Level descriptors		
	Focus	**Use of sources**	**Own knowledge**
7–9	The response is focused on the question.	Clear references are made to the sources, and these references are used effectively as evidence to support the analysis.	Accurate and relevant own knowledge is demonstrated. There is effective synthesis of own knowledge and source material.
4–6	The response is generally focused on the question.	References are made to the sources, and these references are used as evidence to support the analysis.	Where own knowledge is demonstrated, this lacks relevance or accuracy. There is little or no attempt to synthesize own knowledge and source material.
1–3	The response lacks focus on the question.	References to the sources are made, but at this level these references are likely to consist of descriptions of the content of the sources rather than the sources being used as evidence to support the analysis.	No own knowledge is demonstrated or, where it is demonstrated, it is inaccurate or irrelevant.
0	The response does not reach a standard described by the descriptors above.	The response does not reach a standard described by the descriptors above.	The response does not reach a standard described by the descriptors above.

Source: IB history specimen paper

↻ **Reflection**

Reflection

What do you think are the most important words in these markbands? Based on these markbands and in your own words, how would you describe a *good* response to this question?

▶▶ **Assessment tip**

Do not quote directly from the sources at length. Briefly paraphrasing the source shows that you understand the source and does not take up a great deal of time. Identify brief quotes from the sources and indicate from which source they came.

A general discussion or summary of the sources and/or your own knowledge will fall into the 1–3 markband as it does not focus on the question being asked. Therefore, some portion of each paragraph should relate explicitly to the question being asked.

The second element focuses on how well the response uses the sources to answer the question. If the response does not mention or use the sources at all, it will receive a 0 in this element. If a response refers to the sources by simply paraphrasing them it will fall into the 1–3 markband. To achieve beyond this level, a response must include the use of sources. How well a response uses the sources to address the question distinguishes the top two markbands.

The third element revolves around how effectively a response integrates knowledge that is not found in the sources. If a response relies entirely on the information that is in the sources, the response cannot achieve above a 3 in this element. The 4–6 markband describes responses that do have information not included in the sources, but this information might not be completely accurate or relevant. Responses that do not integrate or combine this knowledge with the information from the sources cannot score above this markband. This is why paragraphs should be constructed so that they have both source knowledge and material not included in the sources.

While there is no requirement that you use all the sources when answering the fourth question, it is expected that you refer to at least two of the sources.

What is *best fit*?

When a response demonstrates characteristics from different levels of achievement across two or more elements, markers will use a *best fit* model to determine the overall mark – choosing the level that describes most of the response. For example:

- Focus = 4–6 level
- Sources = 4–6 level
- Knowledge = 4–6 level
- Overall = 5 – the middle of the markband as all the applicable descriptors are from the same markband.

However:

- Focus = 4–6 level
- Sources = 4–6 level
- Knowledge = 7–9 level
- Overall = 6 – the top of the markband as one of the characteristics is from the 7–9 markband.

Here is a sample fourth question and answer. The question refers to the sources E to H, which appear in both section 1.2 (pages 8-9) and section 1.6 (pages 24-25).

QUESTION PRACTICE

Using the sources and your own knowledge, to what extent do you agree with the suggestion that Japanese foreign policy aims up to 1937 were to be achieved through "gradual and peaceful ways" (Source F)? [9]

SAMPLE STUDENT ANSWER

There are various suggestions indicating that the Japanese foreign policy aims up to 1937 were to be achieved through gradual and political means. As Source F suggests, Japan faced various challenges from abroad and had to establish friendly relations with great powers and China in order to strengthen her national power in the East and achieve its long term destiny of becoming the leader of East Asia.

In order to establish peaceful relations with the West, Japan agreed to the Kellogg-Briand pact of 1928 which suggested that countries should not wage war when resolving disputes. Furthermore, Japan took part in the Washington Treaty System of 1920s which included the Nine-Power Treaty that recognized Chinese sovereignty and dependence. Thus, Japan aimed to "establish cordial relations founded on the principles of co-existence and co-prosperity" as Source F mentions. Nonetheless, Japan needed to create a lifeline for its rapidly growing population and needed to create a buffer zone against the USSR. As Source G indicates, "Japan's military strategy aimed at defending itself against the Soviet Union" and hence Japan invaded Manchuria in 1931 and further expanded in China through expressing brutal actions in Nanjing. Although the Japanese government did not allow the occupation of China, the Kwantung Army's independent and aggressive behaviour led to the escalation of the Mukden Incident that created a pretext for the Japanese forces to invade Manchuria. The military influence of the Kwantung Army in Japanese politics, as discussed in Source G, and the public opinion following Japanese expansionist aims caused the army to behave independently of the Japanese government and attack China as displayed in Source H. Despite the Japanese government's attempts to comply with the international law to a certain extent, the Kwantung Army's aggressive and independent attitude caused the international community to view Japan as deceitful. Although I agree that

▲ A thesis statement that clearly focuses on the question.

▲ Source knowledge related to question.

▲ Source knowledge combined with own knowledge.

▲ Source knowledge combined with own knowledge.

▼ Although it does relate back to the question somewhat, this direct quote could have been given some context.

▼ There is some own knowledge here, but it is generalized to the point of questionable relevance.

▼ Good source knowledge with some own knowledge, but limited attempt to tie it back to the question.

▼ Limited context for this knowledge.

▼ Supporting this with specific own knowledge would have strengthened this portion.

▲ A good concluding statement that focuses on the question and addresses the command term "to what extent" by examining both sides of the question.

Japanese government aimed to establish a peaceful foreign policy. I disagree that the foreign policy aims up to 1937 were to be achieved through gradual and peaceful ways.

This response could have achieved 7/9 marks.

1.6   A SAMPLE EXAM PAPER AND RESPONSE

You should be able to:

✔ apply the material in the previous sections to the sources and questions below;

✔ analyse the strengths and weaknesses of the sample below.

Below is a set of sources for prescribed subject 3 as well as questions and responses from a previous exam session. You will recognise these sources as they first appeared in Section 1.2 (pages 8-9). You can test yourself by attempting the questions and then comparing your response to the student sample.

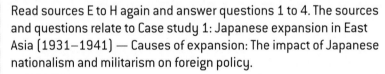

QUESTION PRACTICE

Read sources E to H again and answer questions 1 to 4. The sources and questions relate to Case study 1: Japanese expansion in East Asia (1931–1941) — Causes of expansion: The impact of Japanese nationalism and militarism on foreign policy.

Source E

An extract from a Japanese government statement, "The Fundamental Principles of National Policy" (August 1936).

(1) Japan must strive to eradicate [eliminate] the aggressive policies of the great powers …

(3) … in order to promote Manchukuo's healthy development and to stabilize Japan-Manchukuo national defense, the threat from the north, the Soviet Union, must be eliminated; in order to promote our economic development, we must prepare against Great Britain and the United States and bring about close collaboration between Japan, Manchukuo, and China. In the execution of this policy, Japan must pay due attention to friendly relations with other powers.

(4) Japan plans to promote her racial and economic development in the South Seas, especially in the outlying South Seas area. She plans to extend her strength by moderate and peaceful means without arousing other powers. In this way, concurrently with the firm establishment of Manchukuo, Japan must expect full development and strengthening of her national power.

Source F

William Beasley, a professor of the history of the Far East, writing in the academic book *Japanese Imperialism, 1894–1945* (1987).

Central to the basic propositions was the intention that Japan … must establish cordial [friendly] relations with the peoples of the area founded on the principles of co-existence and co-prosperity. It would also undertake economic expansion on its own account by creating a strong coalition between Japan, Manchukuo and China and by extending its interests in South-East Asia in gradual and peaceful ways. There were some conditions. The army must be given forces in Korea and Kwantung [Guandong] sufficient to deal with any attack from Soviet Russia. The navy must have a fleet capable of maintaining ascendancy in the west Pacific against that of the United States.

Sino-Japanese [Chinese-Japanese] cooperation, designed to detach Nanking [Nanjing] from its communist affiliations [links], though highly desirable must not be allowed to stand in the way of treating north China as a "special region" to be brought into close relationship with Japan and Manchukuo. It was, for example, to provide strategic materials, in order to strengthen their defences against the Soviet Union. As to the south, a gradual and peaceful approach was intended to avert fears in countries of the area concerning Japanese aims …

From the point of view of the ministers in Tokyo, none of this was meant to bring about territorial expansion. They still thought in terms of informal empire, that is, of securing an increase in Japan's privileges through pressure exerted on Asian governments, including that of China.

Source G

Hans van de Ven, a professor of modern Chinese history, writing in the academic book *War and Nationalism in China: 1925–1945* (2003).

By 1933, Japan's military strategy aimed at defending itself against the Soviet Union, China and the British and American navies. Massive investment programmes in the heavy, chemical, and machinery industries followed to give Japan the industrial base to sustain itself in time of war, and also of course to deal with the problems of the Depression. In 1936, Japan stepped up its military expenditures when a new cabinet accepted the build-up of national strength as Japan's highest priority …

Japan therefore developed a strategic doctrine aimed at defending Japan by aggressive offensive operations of limited duration, to be concluded before its major enemies could concentrate their forces in East Asia. To defeat China before such a war was part of this strategy. Worried about war with the Soviet Union and the Western powers, the "removal of China", as the aggressive General Tojo stated in a telegram from Manchuria to Tokyo in early 1937, would eliminate "an important menace from our rear" and release forces for service on more critical fronts. If the military build-up and the political influence of the army in Japanese politics were causes for worry in China, so were the expansionist tendencies of the Kwantung [Guandong] Army in Manchuria.

Source H

John Bernard Partridge, an illustrator and cartoonist, depicts Japan threatening China in an untitled cartoon for the British magazine *Punch* (21 July 1937). Note: The word on the tail is Manchukuo.

S.O.S.

Chinese dragon: I say, do be careful with that sword! If you try to cut off my head I shall really have to appeal to the League again.

1 **a)** What, according to Source E, were the challenges facing Japanese national policy?   [3]

   b) What does Source H suggest about Sino-Japanese [Chinese–Japanese] relations in 1937?   [2]

2 With reference to its origin, purpose, and content, analyse the value and limitations of Source E for a historian studying Japanese foreign policy in East Asia.   [4]

3 Compare and contrast what Sources F and G reveal about Japanese foreign policy aims in East Asia.   [6]

4 Using the sources and your own knowledge, to what extent do you agree with the suggestion that Japanese foreign policy aims up to 1937 were to be achieved through "gradual and peaceful ways" (Source F)?   [9]

SAMPLE STUDENT ANSWER

1 a) According to Source E, Japanese foreign policy had faced the threat of aggressive policies from the great powers, which it strived to eradicate.

Source E also states that the Soviet Union's threat from the north of Japan was also a challenge to foreign policy, and had to be eliminated.

Source E also states that one challenge that they faced was the need to establish friendly relations with other powers such as China and Manchukuo.

Source E also states that one challenge was the extension of Japanese strength through moderate and peaceful means without arousing other powers.

▲ Three valid challenges taken directly from the source.

SAMPLE STUDENT ANSWER

The points in this response are paraphrased and not directly quoted, indicating an understanding of the content.

Note that the question is out of three marks and therefore only requires three valid points, although this response gives four. Also note that as this is the first question, these points do not require much elaboration.

Note that all the information in the response to 1 a) and 1 b) comes directly from the source. The question does not require referral to any material other than the sources.

This response could have achieved 3/3 marks.

b) Source H suggests that China was extremely vulnerable to Japan, as evidenced from the Chinese dragon's neck being exposed to the Japanese warrior's sword, and the dragon looking terrified of the possibility of the Japanese cutting off its head.

Source H also suggests that China was already attacked by Japan, as the tail of the dragon with 'Manchukuo' written on it, suggests that Japan had already taken away Manchukuo from China.

▲ This is a valid point taken directly from the source. The response also explains how it suggests that China was vulnerable to Japan.

Source H also suggests that China had no other defence measures other than to threaten to appeal to the League of Nations as written in the caption, and was the only option that China could use to deter Japan.

▲ This is another valid point taken from the caption of the cartoon. There is some elaboration.

This response could have achieved 2/2 marks.

2 According to its origins, Source E is valuable as it was an extract from a Japanese government statement and would reflect the intended foreign policy goals and ways to achieve them accurately as it came from the Japanese government itself with the information divulged functioning as the official foreign policy stance of the government.

▲ This explains the value associated with the origin of the document.

According to Source E's content, it is valuable as it uses objective language to depict the intentions and aims of the Japanese foreign policy. The source uses recurrent language such as "in order to" and "must" to tie the aims of the Japanese foreign policy closely to the ways in which it would be intended to achieve it, thus is extremely clear in outlining the foreign policy.

▲ A point of value that relates to the tone of the document, but with limited connection to the substance of the content.

According to purpose, source E is limited as it might have been used as a tool to alter the public perception of the Japanese people. The purpose of the Japanese government statement is to lay out its plan of foreign policy that it wishes to portray, and this might deviate from the actual foreign policy that they execute.

▲ The potential of the document to be a tool of propaganda is a valid limitation associated with the purpose.

▼ This limitation of the origin is not well explained.

According to its origin, Source E is limited as it was published in the year of 1936, and the execution of its foreign policy might have been subject to changes over the years, especially since the war had occurred a few years after.

> The response analyses three valid points – one of limitation and two of value. It uses the origin, purpose, and content as evidence.
>
> **This response could have achieved 3/4 marks.**

3 Sources F and G differ in the portrayal of the nature of the Japanese defensive measures. Source F states that Japan would undertake defensive measures through extending its interests in South East Asia in gradual and peaceful ways, while source G states that it aimed at defending Japan by aggressive offensive operations.

▲ Two valid points of contrast explained clearly.

Sources F and G also differ in the portrayal of the nature of the intended relationship between China and Japan. Source G states that the defeat of China was part of Japanese foreign policy aims, while Source F states that Sino-Japanese cooperation was highly desirable, and the defeat of China was not intended although an option.

> This response uses a thematic structure, examining elements of the sources such as expansion, Japanese aims, and the relationship with China.

▲ Another valid point of contrast explained clearly.

Sources F and G also differ on the nature of Japanese expansionist aims. Source F states that the policies were not meant to bring about territorial expansion, while Source G states that the Japanese Kwantung army had expansionist tendencies.

Sources F and G are similar in portraying the Japanese aims against the Soviet Union. Source F states that Japan had to strengthen their defences against the Soviet Union while Source G states that it aimed to defend itself against the Soviet Union, thus are similar.

▲ Three valid similarities explained clearly.

Sources F and G are also similar in portraying the build-up of national strength that Japan was undertaking. Source F states that the Japanese navy must have a strong fleet, and the army must also be given forces. Source G also states that the new cabinet accepted the build of up national strength as Japan's highest priority.

Sources F and G are also similar in portraying Japanese attempts at reviving its economy. Source F states that Japan would

undertake economic expansion while Source G states that Japan
would need to deal with the economic problems of the depression.

Note that each thematic paragraph refers to both sources.

This question is worth six marks and there are six points of compare
and contrast in this response, although that is not strictly necessary to
achieve the highest markband for this question.

This response could have achieved 6/6 marks.

---

4 Japanese foreign policy up till 1937 was largely defined
by her relations with China and investigating its nature is vital
in deciphering the move to global war and its origins, as Japanese
expansionism got gradually more aggressive.

Japanese foreign policy had ostensibly been aimed at defending
herself through the use of peaceful methods. Sources E and F
support this claim. Source E states that Japan had focused on
paying "attention to friendly relations with other powers", and
wanted to achieve "close collaboration between Japan, Manchukuo,
and China." Furthermore, Source E states that Japan "plans to
extend her strength by moderate and peaceful means without
arousing other powers." Source E would accurately represent the
foreign policy aims that Japan had intended to achieve being a
direct statement from the Japanese government. Source F had also
echoed these claims, stating that Japan had aimed to establish
"cordial relations with the peoples of the area founded by co-
existence and co-prosperity", and that it would extend its interest
in "gradual and peaceful ways".

Thus, it can be deduced that Japanese foreign policy had ostensibly
aimed to be gradual and peaceful, based on these sources.
However, in the execution of these policies, Japan was not friendly
or peace-making, as evidenced from Sources G and H's messages.
Source G states that Japanese policies were in fact intended to
"defeat China" and aimed at defending itself against the Chinese,
British, and American navies, not just the Soviet Union. Japan
thus could be seen as having deviated from the aims that it had
ostensibly portrayed as aforementioned. One reason for this would
be that Japan wanted a free hand at issues in the Asiatic region
and wanted minimal Western involvement, thus had ostensibly
provided statements declaring its peaceful aims while plotting

▲ Indicates that the response
will address the command term
to what extent.

▲ A sentence that clearly and
concisely addresses the question.

▲ This paragraph uses source
knowledge from Sources E and F
to address the question, but limited
outside knowledge.

▲ This phrase ties the material
in this paragraph back to the
question, thereby maintaining the
focus.

▲ By including this portion, the
response addresses the command
term *to what extent*.

▲ This paragraph is better at
integrating source knowledge from
Sources G and H with outside
knowledge than the previous
paragraph.

expansionist measures privately. Knowing that tension existed between Britain and the Soviet Union regarding the Munich conference, and that the Western powers were preoccupied with the German expansion led by Hitler, Japan was thus able to devise a façade of wanting to protect itself against the Soviet Union, thus giving a reason for the rapid build-up of military forces in Japan, knowing that Britain and France would most likely not react, due to their mistrust of the Soviets as well.

Source H had also portrayed an instance of Japanese aggression, as the Japanese powers had cut off the tail of the Chinese dragon labelled "Manchukuo", alluding to the Japanese takeover of Manchukuo. The Japanese takeover of Manchukuo was not a manifestation of peace, and was in fact an instance of Japanese aggression, as the Chinese had been attacked by the Japanese, and a brief period of skirmishes saw Japan violently take over Manchukuo. As the Source's caption alludes to, China then appealed to the League of Nations to curb Japanese expansionism into Chinese territory, which was aggressive and against international law. The League was mostly ineffective and allowed for Japan to continue having a military presence in Manchukuo hence allowing the Japanese to have a base near China to launch a violent offensive against.

▼ While there is some outside knowledge here, it is primarily from Source H.

In conclusion, the Japanese foreign policy was ostensibly peaceful and gradual, as intended by the Japanese government. However, in reality, Japan had always intended for an aggressive expansion in the Asiatic region, and the execution of her policy would be able to support this claim. Thus, the statement is largely false as the Japanese had in fact adopted aggressive and violent policies. The manifestation of this could be seen from Japanese historical expansionist agenda, evidenced from her annexation of Korea in 1910 and the Sino-Japanese war.

▲ This is a clear concluding paragraph that refers directly back to the question.

Reflection

What was your overall impression of this response? What are some adjectives that you would use to describe it? How could this response been improved upon? How would you have marked each question in the response?

There is a clear focus on the question. Clear references are made to the sources and these are used as evidence to support the analysis. While some own knowledge is used, this is not sustained throughout the answer.

This response could have achieved 8/9 marks.

2 PAPER 2

You should be able to:

- ✔ describe the structure of paper 2 and its relation to the structure of the world history topics;
- ✔ understand the demands of paper 2 questions;
- ✔ use historical knowledge to answer paper 2 questions;
- ✔ use examples to support a historical argument;
- ✔ provide clear and coherent critical analysis of a historical issue;
- ✔ evaluate different historical perspectives.

2.1   PAPER 2 OVERVIEW

The world history topics and paper 2

Paper 2 is designed to assess the knowledge and skills of the second component of the IB history course, the world history topics. It is therefore important to understand the structure of both of these elements. While the prescribed subjects use source analysis to explore two specific case studies, the world history topics component of the course is broader, giving you the opportunity to study a wide range of historical themes across a much wider span of time.

The world history topics component of the course requires that you study two topics. Each of these topics is structured around themes. Topic 11: Causes and effects of 20th-century wars, for example, focuses on the following themes:

- Causes of war
- Practices of war and their impact on the outcome
- Effects of war.

Each of these themes is, in turn, associated with prescribed content listed in bullet points. For example, the prescribed content for "Practices of war and their impact on the outcome" covers the following:

- Types of war: civil wars; wars between states; guerrilla wars
- Technological developments; air, naval and land warfare
- The extent of the mobilization of human and economic resources
- The influence and/or involvement of foreign powers.

You might notice that no specific war is mentioned. This means that any 20th-century war can be used to explore these general themes and content. The same is true of all the topics. Any appropriate examples can be used to address the themes and prescribed content. Any 20th-century authoritarian regime can be used to explore the themes and content of world history topic 10: Authoritarian states (20th century). Some schools may use Stalin, Mao Zedong, and Hitler to explore the themes and content, while others might use Peron, Castro, and Mussolini.

You should be able to:

- ✔ demonstrate an understanding of paper 2;
- ✔ recognize paper 2's relationship to the world history topics;
- ✔ familiarize yourself with the organization of the questions;
- ✔ understand how the markbands are used to assess your answers.

⟳ Reflection

Which world history topics does your school study? Which examples do you use for each of these topics? Choose two countries in two regions other than your own. What examples might you be studying for the same topics if you were living in each of those countries?

The world history topics explore concepts, themes, and historical material across the globe. As such, it is important to study examples from multiple countries – in fact, it is essential to study examples from more than one region. For this course, the IB has divided the world into four regions: Africa and the Middle East, Asia and Oceania, Europe, and the Americas. A copy of this map will be on the first page of the exam for your reference.

▲ Figure 2.1.1 IB regional map
Source: IB History guide

Note: Although Russia is geographically in both Asia and Europe, for the purposes of paper 2 it is in the Europe region and cannot be used as an Asian example.

The structure of paper 2

Paper 2 has 24 questions – two questions on each of the twelve world history topics. You are required to write on any two questions and each of these questions must be taken from a *different* topic. Some of these questions will require you to examine countries in different regions and therefore it is vital to prepare examples from more than one region.

What happens if you mistakenly answer two questions from the same topic? While both responses will be graded, you will only receive a mark for the higher of the two. For example, from the sample questions on the following pages, if you receive a mark of 10/15 for question 13 and 12/15 for question 14 (both from topic 7: Origins, development, and impact of industrialization) you would receive 12/30 for paper 2.

The questions on paper 2 tend to be broad. They will not ask you about any specific example. Rather, the questions will ask about themes or prescribed content from the subject guide. You are free to use any appropriate example to answer the question. For example, there will be no questions on the causes of the First World War. Instead the question could ask about the causes of 20th-century wars and you can use the First World War, or any other 20th-century war, to answer it.

You will get 90 minutes to complete paper 2. As each question is worth 15 marks and weighted equally, you should aim to take roughly 45 minutes answering each question. As with all IB exams – except multiple-choice exams – you will get 5 minutes of reading time before you begin that is not included in the 90 minutes. You are not permitted to do any writing during these 5 minutes, so you should use the time to read the questions you could potentially answer and begin to order your thoughts.

>> **Assessment tip**

Paper 2 is physically organized by numbered topics and the course requires you study two topics. Do not waste time reading the entire exam paper. Begin reading the questions on the topics you have studied. For example, if your class has studied topic 10: Authoritarian states (20th century) and topic 12: The Cold War, start reading at question 19.

Below is an example of how the questions appear in the actual exam. These questions come from the May 2017 exam.

Topic 6: Causes and effects of Early Modern wars (1500–1750)

11 Evaluate the importance of religion in causing two wars.

12 "Technological developments were the most significant factor in determining the outcome of Early Modern wars." Discuss with reference to two wars.

Topic 7: Origins, development, and impact of industrialization (1750–2005)

13 "Industrialization was entirely the result of technological development." Discuss with reference to two countries, each from a different region.

14 Evaluate the social and political impact of industrialization in one country.

The questions on paper 2 will be set on the themes, prescribed content, and/or the contextual material that is at the beginning of each topic in the subject guide. It is therefore vital that you prepare all these elements for the exam.

Marking paper 2

Paper 2 is marked according to a single set of markbands that apply to all questions.

▼ Table 2.1.1 Paper 2 markbands

Marks	Level descriptor
13–15	Responses are clearly focused, showing a high degree of awareness of the demands and implications of the question. Responses are well structured and effectively organized.
	Knowledge of the world history topic is accurate and relevant. Events are placed in their historical context, and there is a clear understanding of historical concepts.
	The examples that the student chooses to discuss are appropriate and relevant, and are used effectively to support the analysis/evaluation. The response makes effective links and/or comparisons (as appropriate to the question).
	The response contains clear and coherent critical analysis. There is evaluation of different perspectives, and this evaluation is integrated effectively into the answer. All, or nearly all, of the main points are substantiated, and the response argues to a consistent conclusion.
10–12	The demands of the question are understood and addressed. Responses are generally well structured and organized, although there is some repetition or lack of clarity in places.
	Knowledge of the world history topic is mostly accurate and relevant. Events are placed in their historical context, and there is some understanding of historical concepts.
	The examples that the student chooses to discuss are appropriate and relevant, and are used to support the analysis/evaluation. The response makes effective links and/or comparisons (as appropriate to the question).
	The response contains critical analysis, which is mainly clear and coherent. There is some awareness and evaluation of different perspectives. Most of the main points are substantiated and the response argues to a consistent conclusion.

Marks	Level descriptor
7–9	The response indicates an understanding of the demands of the question, but these demands are only partially addressed. There is an attempt to follow a structured approach.
	Knowledge of the world history topic is partly accurate and relevant. Events are generally placed in their historical context.
	The examples that the student chooses to discuss are appropriate and relevant. The response makes links and/or comparisons (as appropriate to the question).
	The response moves beyond description to include some analysis or critical commentary, but this is not sustained.
4–6	The response indicates some understanding of the demands of the question. While there may be an attempt to follow a structured approach, the response lacks clarity and coherence.
	Knowledge of the world history topic is demonstrated, but lacks accuracy and relevance. There is a superficial understanding of historical context.
	The student identifies specific examples to discuss, but these examples are vague or lack relevance.
	There is some limited analysis, but the response is primarily narrative/descriptive in nature rather than analytical.
1–3	There is little understanding of the demands of the question. The response is poorly structured or, where there is a recognizable essay structure, there is minimal focus on the task.
	Little knowledge of the world history topic is present.
	The student identifies examples to discuss, but these examples are factually incorrect, irrelevant or vague.
	The response contains little or no critical analysis. The response may consist mostly of generalizations and poorly substantiated assertions.
0	Answers do not reach a standard described by the descriptors above.

Source: IB history specimen paper

 Reflection

Examining the markbands

Take some time to read through the markbands. What do you notice about how each markband is structured? What general categories are the markbands evaluating? What are some of the important words in each descriptor?

In your reflection you may have noticed that each markband evaluates the same dimensions of an answer:

- Focus and structure
- Knowledge and context
- Examples and links/comparisons
- Analysis, perspectives, and conclusion.

The rest of this chapter will look at each of these dimensions in turn.

2.2   FOCUS AND STRUCTURE

You should be able to:

✔ understand the demands of paper 2 questions;

✔ structure your response effectively;

✔ use command terms;

✔ write an effective thesis statement.

Paper 2 questions

As we discussed in the last section, the world history topics are organized around themes and prescribed content, not specific examples. This means that the questions on paper 2 tend to be more broad or general in nature than the questions on paper 1 or paper 3. The first thing you do, once you have decided which question you are going to answer, is to "unpack" it – pull it apart to understand what it is asking. Here are the parts of a typical paper 2 question:

- Command term
- Themes/content
- Restrictions.

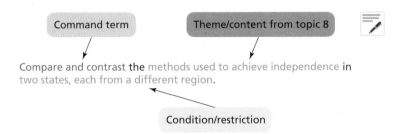

▲ Figure 2.2.1 The parts of a typical paper 2 question

Sometimes the question will use a quotation to focus the question:

> "The expansion of early modern colonial empires was motivated by economic factors." Discuss with reference to two early modern colonial empires.

In all these cases, it is important to consider all the terms in the question and this includes any quotation that is included. Likewise, pay attention to conjunctions such as *and*. If a question uses the word *and*, then both elements must be addressed in the response.

Command terms

All paper 2 questions will contain a command term and this is the key to understanding the nature of the task. These will be the same command terms used in the fourth question of paper 1. Here are some points to keep in mind when addressing these command terms in paper 2.

Compare and contrast questions will require you to do both – compare and contrast – that is, you will need to look at both similarities and differences in order to properly address the question.

Evaluation questions involve making a judgment based on strengths *and* weaknesses. This means that you need to include all three of these elements in your response. You should also explain the rationale behind your judgment – be explicit.

To what extent … questions require you to assess features on both sides of an issue. For example, consider the following question:

> "Superpower rivalry in Europe and Asia between 1943 and 1949 led to a breakdown of the grand alliance." To what extent do you agree with this statement?

You would need to provide points on *both* sides of the question – when between 1943 and 1949 superpower rivalry did and did not contribute to the breakdown of the alliance, and which side the greatest amount of evidence supports. Furthermore, a proper focus on this question would need to discuss developments in both Europe *and* Asia. If only one of these elements was addressed, the response could not achieve full marks.

>> **Assessment tip**

When answering *To what extent* ... questions, it is important to maintain a focus on what the question is asking. The question *To what extent were economic policies important to the maintenance of power in one authoritarian state?* requires that the focus of your response be economic policies. If you stated that economic policies were important only to a limited extent and then spent most of the response discussing other policies, you would not be seen as focusing on the question.

This particular question also contains a specific time period. When this is the case, the events discussed must fit within the set period. It is permissible, however, to discuss broad implications of an event that go beyond the time period as long as the event you are using for the example itself occurred within the period. For example, for the question above, you could use the creation of NATO in 1949, even though much of the tension caused by this event happened after the time parameters of the question – 1949. In some cases, there are time parameters implicit in the question based on the world history topic itself. For example, topic 11: Causes and effects of 20th-century wars or topic 9: Evolution and development of democratic states (1848–2000). In topic 11 the wars that you use as examples must have occurred in the 20th century. It is acceptable to use *causes* of those 20th-century wars, however, that may have happened before the 20th century. For instance, if you are answering a question on the causes of the First World War, it is permissible to discuss the Anglo-German naval arms race even though it started in the 19th century. In terms of topic 9, the democratic states had to "emerge" in the given time period (1848–2000) to be an appropriate example.

Response structure

The first dimension of the paper 2 markbands assesses focus *and* the structure of your response. While there are many effective ways to structure a history response, all should have three basic elements:

- Introduction
- Body
- Conclusion.

The introduction

The introduction lays out your understanding of the question. This is where you indicate that you understand what the command term requires and that you will use appropriate examples. The introduction is also where you can lay out some brief context of the topic. However, resist the urge to write extensively on the background of the topic – you only have about 45 minutes to complete the question.

The introduction is also where you indicate what your answer to the question will be. This is called your thesis or thesis statement. Although it can be positioned anywhere in the introduction, it is often placed at the end to lead the reader into the body of the response. Thesis statements have several components:

Thesis = Answer to the question + a qualifier + a blueprint

The answer to the question is your main position on the question. The qualifier is a potential counter argument to your main position. The blueprint is an indication of the examples you will use to support your position.

Consider the following question:

To what extent did industrialization in two countries rely upon developments in transportation?

A potential thesis could be:

Transportation played an important role in the development of industrialization in Canada and Germany, although other factors such as available labour also played a role.

Note that by looking at transportation as well as other factors, the command term *To what extent …* has been addressed. The thesis then provides the focus for the rest of your response. Each paragraph you write should, in some way, relate back to it. In that way, it also serves as a miniature outline for the response.

Or consider this question:

> Evaluate the impact of two 20th-century wars on the role and status of women.

A thesis might be:

The First World War expanded the role of women in the workforce, though these changes were short-lived and did little to change the status of women in British and French society. The Spanish Civil War changed the role and status of women during the course of the war, but these changes were reversed once Franco and the Nationalists won the war.

Notice that the thesis can be multiple sentences.

QUESTION PRACTICE

> To what extent did economic factors contribute to the emergence of two authoritarian states, each from a different region?

SAMPLE STUDENT ANSWER

Economic factors contributed to the rise of Nazi Germany from 1919 to 1934 and the rise of Communist China from 1921 to 1949. Other factors that may be considered are the use of force by the Nazis and the Communist Party of China (CPC) and each state's leader's personal ability, being Adolf Hitler and Mao Zedong. Ultimately economic factors contributed to the emergence of both states to a larger extent as the prior economic weakness drove the people to support the Nazis and the CPC.

▲ Content focus of question.

▲ Appropriate examples indicating an understanding of the question.

▲ "To what extent…" understood in that both economic factors and other factors (leader's personal ability and use of force) are mentioned.

In the last sentence in this introduction, the thesis = the answer to the question.

The body

The body of the response is a series of paragraphs that provide detailed historical evidence that supports your answer as laid out in the thesis. There are any number of ways to order this evidence. One effective method is to lay out your qualifier or counter argument first. Use the rest of the paragraphs to focus on your main position, ordering them from weakest to strongest. Each paragraph should start with a general statement or an assertion setting up the main point of the paragraph.

This should be followed by specific and detailed pieces of historical evidence that supports the topic sentence. The paragraph should also contain statements that explicitly link the evidence in the paragraph to the thesis – and therefore to the question.

Conclusion

The purpose of the conclusion is to summarize what you have argued in the rest of the answer. While this may seem redundant, a properly written conclusion can refocus the readers' mind on the overall argument of the response and therefore contribute to the overall persuasiveness of the answer. This summary can also refocus the argument back to the question being asked.

A note on structuring a *compare-and-contrast* response

As when addressing the third question in paper 1, you should structure your answers to *compare-and-contrast* questions in paper 2 using an integrated rather than an "end-on" approach. This means that rather than discussing each of the elements being compared in turn, combining an analysis of both elements is a stronger approach. Section 2.4 has more information on structuring *compare-and-contrast* responses.

The markbands

The first dimension of the markbands assesses the focus and structure of your response.

▼ Table 2.2.1 How the markbands assess focus and structure

Level	Focus and structure
13–15	Responses are clearly focused, showing a high degree of awareness of the demands and implications of the question.
	Responses are well structured, balanced, and effectively organized.
10–12	The demands of the question are understood and addressed.
	Responses are generally well structured and organized, although there is some repetition or lack of clarity in places.
7–9	The response indicates an understanding of the demands of the question, but these demands are only partially addressed.
	There is an attempt to follow a structured approach.
4–6	The response indicates some understanding of the demands of the question.
	While there may be an attempt to follow a structured approach, the response lacks clarity and coherence.
1–3	There is little understanding of the demands of the question.
	The response is poorly structured or, where there is a recognizable essay structure, there is minimal focus on the task.

Source: IB history specimen paper

The 1–3 markband in this dimension applies to responses that make very limited reference to the command terms or content of the question, or responses that do not indicate any real understanding of the command terms. A low-markband response does not resemble an essay response. For example, it may consist of a single paragraph.

In a response in the 4–6 markband, you can start to see the structure of an essay emerge. There are generally paragraphs, introduction, and a conclusion, but the overall argument is difficult to follow. Most of the historical material in the answer comes from the correct world history topic and it discusses states, events, and/or leaders that are appropriate to the question.

To reach the 7–9 markband in this dimension, answers must clearly show that you know the command terms in the question and what content and restrictions are appropriate. While the response indicates that you may know what to answer, responses in the 7–9 markband do not fully answer these requirements. For example, if a question asks for economic and social policies and you indicate in your introduction that you will examine these, but only deal with economic policies in detail in the rest of the response, it can fall into this markband for focus and structure. Another situation that could put a response into this markband in the focus and structure dimension is if the introduction indicates that you will examine the merits on both sides of a *To what extent …* question, but then only look at evidence on one side of the issue.

Responses that fall into the 10–12 markband for this dimension both understand the command term and the appropriate content and carry through with this understanding by addressing the demands of the question throughout the rest of the response. The structure is easy to follow despite minor flaws such as repetition.

In the top markband for this dimension, 13–15, responses not only understand the command terms and appropriate content, but address them in depth, discussing elements that might not be immediately obvious in the question. The structure is not just easy to follow, but enhances the response and makes the argument stronger. This can be accomplished by including and refuting counter-arguments, ordering your evidence from weakest to strongest, and including a conclusion that not only summarizes the argument, but adds to it.

QUESTION PRACTICE

Choose two or three of the following questions and write a brief outline for each. Once you have done that, write an introduction for each to indicate that you understand the demands of the question.

1 With reference to two societies, compare and contrast the treatment of religious minorities.

2 With reference to two wars, to what extent do you agree that competition for resources was the main factor contributing to the outbreak of conflict?

3 To what extent did external factors rather than internal factors contribute to the growth of two independence movements?

4 Evaluate the impact of domestic crises on the development of two democratic states.

5 Evaluate the impact of the mobilization of human and economic resources upon the outcome of one 20th-century war.

6 Evaluate the impact of two leaders, each from a different region, on the course of the Cold War.

QUESTION PRACTICE

Evaluate the impact of the mobilization of human and economic resources upon the outcome of one 20th-century war.   (15)

SAMPLE STUDENT ANSWER

▲ Appropriate example.

▲ Some context indicated here.

▲ Content focus of question.

▲ A qualifier.

World War 2 (WW2) was a war between the Allies consisting of Britain, France, the USSR and the USA, and the Axis Powers, consisting of Germany, Italy and Japan, from 1939 to 1945. Mobilization of human and economic resources contributed to the Allied victory, while technological developments and tactical ability also played a role. Ultimately, the successful mobilization of human and economic resources had the greatest impact as this allowed the Allies to sustain a continued attack on the Axis and emerge victorious, as opposed to the weak mobilization by the Axis.

In the last sentence of the introduction, thesis = answer to the question with a blueprint.

▲ Introductory sentence/ assertion related to the question.

▲ Detailed material related to topic sentence and question.

▲ Concluding sentence tying paragraph back to thesis/question.

Mobilization of human and economic resources can be seen in the Operation Barbarossa from 1942-1944 as seen from poor German mobilization and strong Soviet mobilization. Germany planned to invade Russia in 1942. However in 1942 it was running on a shortage of resources, such as iron and oil, hindering its ability to continue to produce tanks. Although it started with 300,000 tanks, by 1943, it was unable to replace its tanks due to slow production rate. This was also due to the Nazi's belief that women were meant to be homemakers and Germany's workforce was comparably weaker to the Allies that mobilized women. The Soviets on the other hand, had a 10 million strong workforce and the strong industrialization from their five-year plans in 1929 and 1935 meant that it had a strong industrial base. Hence this allowed the USSR to sustain a defence from 1942 to 1944 and by 1944, the Germans were too weak to attack anymore, being surrounded by Soviet tanks during the battle of Kiev. After this, the Germans were unable to go on the offensive.

The following paragraph contains the counter argument.

▼ Limited detailed support in this paragraph.

However, the German failure at Operation Barbarossa may have been due to tactical weakness as well. The German Blitzkreig tactic of combined tank and infantry was inefficient in the large geographical landscape of Russia, with tanks travelling thrice as fast as foot soldiers. The sickle stick approach of a three-front invasion also meant that forces were divided and the Germans were unable to have a focused attack on the USSR.

However the Germans may have won even despite tactical failures. The USSR also did not show much tactical prowess but their sheer military force from efficient mobilization allowed them to defeat Germany.

Technological developments also played a contribution to the war, particularly in the Pacific in the battle of Midway in 1942. The Americans had successfully cracked the Japanese naval codes, hence predicting their attack and successfully preparing a counter attack. The Americans also utilised recent naval developments such as hedgehog depth charges that detonated at a radius of 30 miles and Oboe-frequencies which sent a flurry of signals on Japanese radar. Although Japan was on the offensive, Japan lost 4 aircraft carriers and 6 submarines while the US only lost 1 aircraft carrier and 1 submarine. This victory over Japan allowed the US to even take Midway Islands that was a key base in the Pacific Ocean, allowing the US to go on a tighter offensive against Japan and come out victorious.

However, the ultimate deciding factor of the battle in the Pacific would have been atomic bombs that the US dropped on Japan in Hiroshima and Nagasaki, killing 50,000 each. While a technological development, this would not have been possible without strong US mobilization of resources. Being the strongest economy in the world, the US had enough economic resources to engage in the Manhattan Project. Their GDP was twice that of Britain and France's and this allowed them to discover the atomic bomb, hence showing how mobilization of human and economic resources were necessary for technological developments, having the greatest impact on Allied victory.

Tactical ability was also a contributing factor as seen in the 1940 Battle of Britain. Having overtaken France and most of Europe, Germany set its sights on defeating Britain through the use of its air force. Planes were sent to bomb Britain and weaken it prior to an Axis invasion. However, the Germans made the critical mistake of bombing civilians instead of key industrial targets. This allowed the British to sustain a strong counter-attack and eventually defeat the Germans.

However, Britain's key mobilization of resources has to be accounted for in this victory. Although the Germans bombed civilians, this did not dampen morale and the British also used this a propaganda to encourage civilian work in war production.

▲ Topic sentence/assertion related to the question.

▲ Detailed material related to topic sentence and question.

▲ Concluding/analysis tying paragraph back to thesis/question and addressing "impact".

▲ Topic sentence/assertion related to the question.

▼ Limited detailed support.

▲ Concluding/analysis tying paragraph back to thesis/question and addressing "impact".

▲ Material relating directly back to thesis/question.

▼ Very limited discussion of "human resources" element of question.

Although the Germans had a ratio of 3:1 of planes compared to the British, the British dedication of 50% of its economy, key management of rations and its mobilization of 80% of women meant that the British plane production outstripped the Germans and eventually the Germans had to cease their attack on Britain due to the shortage of resources. Hence, while German tactical weakness was present, victory for Britain would not have been possible without successful mobilization and this victory hence allows the Allies to go on the offensive and eventually win the war.

In conclusion, successful mobilization had the greatest impact as it not only allowed the Allies to have a sustained defence but it amplified their technological developments and helped them counter tactical weakness by the Germans.

▲ This paragraph ends with a connection to the "impact" element of the question.

▲ Concise conclusion restating thesis.

Overall, this response understands the demands of the question, but only addresses economic mobilization in depth, and therefore only partially addresses the question.

This response could have achieved 8/15 marks.

2.3   KNOWLEDGE AND CONTEXT

You should be able to:

✔ understand the role of knowledge in a paper 2 response;

✔ prepare for writing paper 2;

✔ use concepts to answer paper 2 questions.

Historical knowledge

The second dimension of paper 2 assessment is *knowledge and context*. The knowledge required here is specifically historical knowledge. It is a vital element in any historical argument as it is information on the people and events of the past that is used as evidence. Simply put, it is the facts of history.

Obviously, not just any historical facts will do. This dimension of the markbands assesses how well you understand these facts and how well you use them to support your answer to the question. They must therefore be both relevant and accurate.

It is important to understand the difference between assertions and support for this paper. An assertion is a statement that is not demonstrably correct. It is an opinion or a statement of position rather than a fact. To be useful in historical arguments and therefore in paper 2 responses, assertions need to be supported by actual historical facts. In that way, assertions and support need each other. Without support, assertions are just unverifiable generalizations about the past.

Without assertions, historical facts are just random collections of information unconnected to larger truths we can learn from history – in other words, trivia. This is why paper 2 requires assertions that are supported by accurate facts and that both are relevant to the questions being asked.

QUESTION PRACTICE

"The effects of war on the role and status of women were mostly beneficial." Discuss with reference to two wars.

SAMPLE STUDENT ANSWER

Before the First World War women were just handling the household and taking care of the children and the home while the husband made money. When the war started and the men went to fight at the Front women took over the "men jobs" in factories to make more weapons or do the jobs that were left over on the land like farming. Because men were at war, women had a greater public influence as they were the working women now. This rise in public attention and influence led to the creation of women organizations that protest for Women's Suffrage. Their public engagement gave them the right to protest more aggressively. After the war ended and the men returned from war the women had to leave their working place and the men took back their jobs. It was still frowned upon in the society if a woman worked.

▲ Assertion.

▲ Assertion.

▲ Assertion.

Historical concepts

One of the key elements of an IB education is that it is conceptually based. The IB describes concepts as "big powerful ideas that have relevance both within and across subject areas." In some ways, it is the concepts that make the history we are studying meaningful rather than just interesting. The *knowledge and context* dimension of the paper 2 markbands is where your understanding and application of these concepts is assessed.

Continuity: While much of the study of history concentrates on how and why society changes, in many ways this only has meaning if we understand what has not changed. It is therefore important to find and understand what does not change during a period of history. For example, knowing about the elements of Tsarist Russia that were maintained after the Bolshevik revolution helps us understand that revolution more fully.

Change: Inherent in the study of history is the attempt to understand how and why change happens. IB history encourages you to make judgments on the extent of change, as well as the processes that both brought about the change and those forces that opposed it.

Causation: Central to the study of history is the desire to understand why events in the past happened. This is an incredibly complex task as most events are the result of diverse and interconnected sets of actions. Some developments or actions were more significant than others in explaining the cause of events, and as students of history we need to able to make judgments about which of these are more important and substantiate these judgments with evidence.

Concept link

What are the historical concepts that we focus on in the IB?

- Continuity
- Change
- Causation
- Consequence
- Significance
- Perspective.

Consequence: One of the reasons we study history is to try to know how the past influences subsequent events in order get a better understanding how our present society functions. What are the long- and short-term effects of a key event?

Significance: The study of history is more than listing the events of the past. Historians must make judgments on what events, actions, and records are more important than others in studying an aspect of history. We must constantly ask why some events and explanations are considered significant. Why are some events, people, or developments considered more significant than others in understanding the past? Is this justified?

Perspective: Historical narratives, judgments, and explanations can differ according to who is experiencing them. A complete view of the past, or at least as complete as we can get, requires that we examine it from multiple perspectives. How do these perspectives compare? These can be individual perspectives or the perspective of groups such as minorities or women.

These perspectives often work together to form a more complete understanding of a historical event. For example, depending on the perspective, an event or action may be viewed as hugely significant or totally insignificant. Likewise, the consequences of an event may be looked at differently depending on the perspectives of the groups involved.

What is context?

In short, context is the facts that exist outside the main event being studied that are required to understand that event. While not the focus of the response, the context provides the background information that helps make sense of that focus. For example, if the focus of a question is the economic policies of an authoritarian state and the chosen example is Nazi Germany, the context of the Second World War is important to understand Nazi economic policies from 1939 to 1945. Having said that, the response must not only focus on the military events of the Second World War.

Preparing for paper 2

One challenging aspect of paper 2 revolves around the idea that while the questions are rather broad or general in nature, they require detailed historical knowledge to answer well. This is compounded by the fact that the scope of the material in the world history topics is rather extensive. In other words, there is a great deal of historical material that you have to learn for the exam. So how do you do that?

Plan, plan, plan

One aspect of IB history that makes it very difficult is the fact that there is a great deal of history to cover. This can be made more manageable by finding overlap for material and examples that work for more than one element of the assessment. It cannot be revised or studied properly in one or two sessions. The more you can break the material into smaller bits and prepare these over a long period, the more likely you are to remember it. Take the number of days you have to prepare and divide the material up among those days. It is always good to leave time at the end to prepare mock exams and review material about which you are unclear.

> ↻ **Reflection**
>
> For the two or three questions you wrote outlines and introductions for, in the Question practice in section 2.2, explain how you might incorporate two of the historical concepts above into the outline.

> ≫ **Assessment tip**
>
> No single bullet point or content in the curriculum is any more important than others. Exam questions can be set on any of the content in the subject guide, so you will need to prepare all of this material. If you start to try to guess what will be asked, you run the risk of not being able to answer enough questions.

Write, write, write (do not type)

When studying/revising for exams, simply reading over your notes is not enough. Physically writing out study notes helps with retention of information. It requires that you process what you are writing and this helps you to remember it. Typing does not have the same effect because proficient typists process letters and key strokes independently of the word or phrase being typed, which means they can type a whole paragraph without understanding what it means … and understanding is the whole point of preparing for an exam. Practising your handwriting can also help make it more legible on the actual exam.

Collect all the information you have on the section you are preparing – class notes, handouts, textbook information. Use these to prepare bullet-point notes on the section in your own words. Read these points over several times and then attempt to write them from memory. Check this re-writing against your original study notes. Repeat until you can re-write them to your satisfaction.

Memory dump

Once your five minutes of reading time prior to the exam is complete and you have chosen which questions you are going to answer, use a piece of scrap paper provided for you to write down as much information as you can remember that relates to the questions you have chosen. Once these facts and ideas are down on the paper, you can simply refer to them when you need them and not worry about having to remember them later in the exam. As you remember other ideas or facts as you progress, add them to the memory dump.

Colour-coding and shape-coding

Categorize the material you are studying by colour- or shape-coding can help to make it easier to recall when you are sitting down to write your paper. For example, when preparing material on Mao Zedong as an example of a 20th-century authoritarian regime, you might highlight all the information on his use of force in one colour. This helps our brains to distinguish between different categories of information.

The markbands

The second dimension of the markbands assesses the *knowledge and context* of your response.

> **Reflection**
>
> Make a study/revision plan. Look ahead to your next exam session. How much time will you have to prepare? Remember to consider your other IB subjects as well. Divide all the topics, themes, examples, and content up among those available days. Where can you find efficiencies, or overlap of material, that can be used for each of papers 1, 2, and 3?

▼ Table 2.3.1 How the markbands assess *knowledge and context*

Marks	Knowledge and context
13–15	Knowledge of the world history topic accurate and relevant.
	Events are placed in their historical context and there is a clear understanding of historical concepts.
10–12	Knowledge of the world history topic is mostly accurate and relevant.
	Events are placed in their historical context and there is some understanding of historical concepts.
7–9	Knowledge of the world history topic is partly accurate and relevant.
	Events are generally placed in their historical context.

Source: IB history specimen paper

Reflection

What are the key terms used to measure the quality of the knowledge and context? How could you use your own words to describe answers that fall in the lower markbands (1–3 to 4–6)? What about those at the top end of the markbands?

Answers: Little knowledge, partly accurate, mostly accurate, generally placed in context, placed in context, accurate understanding of concepts

Marks	Knowledge and context
4–6	Knowledge of the world history topic is demonstrated but lacks accuracy and relevance.
	There is superficial understanding of historical context.
1–3	Little knowledge of the world history topic is present.

Responses that fall in the 1–3 markband for this dimension have very few accurate historical facts. If there is material from history, it is not related to the world history topic on which the question is focusing.

In the 4–6 markband for this dimension, historical information is present, but this information is mostly incorrect. Where there are accurate historical facts in the answer, it is not clear how these facts are related to the question being asked. Any mention of context is scant without any direct relation to the knowledge that is presented.

An answer that is placed in the 7–9 markband for this dimension has about as much accurate historical information as it does inaccurate historical information. It should be clear how most of this information relates to the question being asked. There is an overall, rather than a precise, understanding of the relevant context and how it fits with the material used to answer the question.

There can be inaccuracies in a response that reaches the 10–12 markband, but the majority of the material in the answer must be correct. There is context included and it is clear how it relates to the material. This is the first markband that mentions the historical concepts. At the 10–12 level, this understanding of concepts can be explicit or implied. This understanding does not have to include all the concepts.

In the 13–15 markband, responses use accurate historical material that is relevant to the question. Any inaccuracies are insignificant in proportion to the overall complexity of the response and the argument being made. In other words, answers do not have to be 100 per cent accurate to be placed in this markband, but inaccuracies must be minor, inconsequential, and few.

Reflection

Return to the outlines you made in the Question practice in section 2.2. What is the relevant context for each?

QUESTION PRACTICE

"Confrontation rather than reconciliation ended the Cold War."
Discuss with reference to the period from 1980 to 1991. [15]

SAMPLE STUDENT ANSWER

▲ "Confrontation" element of question understood.

▲ Blueprint.

It is periodically argued that confrontation rather than reconciliated ended the Cold War. This claim is often made by Reagan victory school historians who emphasise the success of Reagan's aggressive policies in bringing the Soviet Union to its knees in 1991. However, this claim is unsubstantiated. For one, it neglects to consider the long term economic and ideological crises within the Soviet Union which allowed a short term trigger to cause the demise of the state. Secondly, it disregards the policies of Gorbachev in ending the war; policies implemented neither as a result of short term confrontation, nor reconciliation.

In this case, the entire second half of the introduction serves as the thesis.

The economic and ideological crises within the Soviet Union were the long term cause of the end of the cold war. These crises manifested themselves between the period of 1980 to 1991. The economic situation was pressing. The inherent nature of the communist system had in part caused many unresolved problems; low incentive to work stemming from the lack of a profit motive led to low worker productivity, and the emphasis on heavy industry led to a lack of consumer goods. Annual GDP growth in the 1980s was at 2% compared to 6% in the 1960s. Additionally an ideological breakdown was occurring as citizens lost faith in Marxist Leninist thought. Indeed, Soviet general Dmitri Volkogonov wrote famously "If Lenin was such a genius, how come none of his predictions came to be true?". This growing resistance to communism was evident also in growing unrest in the satellite states of the USSR. It was in these conditions, and these conditions only, that actions of the United States – whether they be confrontational or reconciliatory - could cause the end of the Cold War. As John Lewis Gaddis wrote, "the Soviet Union was a sandpile waiting to collapse." It is sometimes argued that the confrontational policies of Ronald Reagan caused the ultimate implosion.

Reagan's aggressive foreign policies put substantive pressure on the Soviet Union, but did not ultimately prove most significant in destabilising the regime. Ronald Reagan, elected to power in 1980, began pursuing an unforgiving foreign policy in 1982. He increased the proportion of the budget spent on the military by 17%, and launched the strategic defence initiative, a program that aimed to put missiles in space. These policies were intended to economically "squeeze" the Soviet Union until she capitulated. Reagan also waged an ideological war; he denounced communism tirelessly in nationwide speeches, calling the USSR an "evil empire". Reagan victory school historians argue that these uncompromising, confrontational policies caused the end of the Soviet Union and thus the Cold War. However these

▲ Historical context.

▲ Awareness of historical concept of "change".

▲ Explicit awareness of the historical concept of "significance".

historians overstate their case. Indeed the initial Soviet response to the 1982 increase in arms spreading was not to capitulate, but to enter peace talks. This is the second phenomenon which undermines Reagan victory school claims; Reagan's policies were not as confrontational as things appeared. In fact, over the period of 1980 to 1991, there were many peace talks between Gorbachev and Reagan, ending in the signing of the 1987 INF treaty. There was even a natural gas pipeline built between the USSR and the US in the 1980s. Evidently the end of the Cold War was not due to Reagan's confrontational policies. It was also, however, not entirely due to the reconciliation talks. Ultimately the short term trigger was Gorbachev's two policies. Glasnost and Perestroika.

The grain of sand that caused the "sandpile" of the Soviet Union to collapse were Gorbachev's economic and political policies. These were implemented not due to the confrontational stance of the United States, or even due to the reconciliatory peace talks, but rather due to Gorbachev's ability to recognise the underlying economic and ideological weaknesses of his nation. Perestroika was intended to give new life to the economy, it involved the prioritisation of certain land, the invitation for foreign direct inflows, and the liberalisation of economic policies. Glasnost, "openness", was intended to reduce the ideological crisis by reducing censorship and allowing freedom of speech. Ultimately these two policies brought the collapse of the Soviet Union. They led to a wildfire of free speech, the formation of new political parties, and protest across Eastern Europe. This unrest was brought to bear in 1989, when all across the satellite states, communist governments toppled. In Poland the trade union Solidarity won the partially free elections of 1989, and later in the year, nationwide protests in East Germany led to the toppling of the Berlin wall. As the Soviet Union crumbled, Gorbachev refused to intervene with his Red Army, and in 1991, he resigned. The Soviet Union ceased to exist.

Evidently, the end of the Cold War was caused by a myriad of interlocking factors. The most prominent factors were the economic issues and loss of faith in the regime seen following 1980. However this underlying cause of the end of the Cold War was compounded by the attempts of one man to remedy

▲ Explicit awareness of the historical concept of "causation".

▲ Clear link back to the question here.

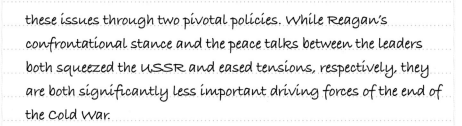

these issues through two pivotal policies. While Reagan's confrontational stance and the peace talks between the leaders both squeezed the USSR and eased tensions, respectively, they are both significantly less important driving forces of the end of the Cold War.

This response could have achieved 12/15 marks.

2.4 EXAMPLES AND LINKS

You should be able to:

✔ use appropriate and relevant examples to support your analysis;

✔ structure a comparative response.

Examples

While the *knowledge and context* dimension assesses the accuracy of your historical knowledge, the *examples and links* dimension of the markbands evaluates how well you use this to support the analysis and arguments you are making in relation to the question.

Appropriate?

As we mentioned, the world history topics stipulate what content and themes you must study; they do not, however, specify what examples you can use in your studies. The nature of the topic does, however, put some parameters on what is "appropriate".

Topic 7: Origins, development, and impact of industrialization (1750–2005): Apart from the obvious fact that your examples must be countries that industrialized between 1750 and 2005, it is important to remember that you need not know all aspects of industrialization throughout this entire time period. For example, if you are studying industrialization in Canada, you need only study the span of time that allows you to understand the themes and content. Studying too wide a time frame makes it difficult to go into enough depth or detail to score well on this dimension.

Topic 8: Independence movements (1800–2000): In all world history topics, the themes and content is preceded by a paragraph of introductory material. This material is part of the required content for the world history topic and can form the basis of a paper 2 exam question. The first sentence in the introduction material for topic 8 is "This theme focuses on the emergence of new states in the 19th and 20th centuries". The word *emergence* is important in this and other topics.

To be considered as appropriate, the movement needs to have been successful in gaining independence in the time period. The Basque independence movement would, therefore, not be an appropriate example, whereas the Indian independence movement would be.

Likewise, the introductory material notes that "the focus of this topic is specifically on movements seeking independence from a foreign power". This means that the efforts of movements in Soviet Bloc countries such as Poland and Czechoslovakia to end communism are not appropriate examples, nor would Argentine efforts to end the dictatorship in the 1980s be acceptable, but Algerian efforts to gain independence from France would be appropriate. To prepare well for answering questions on this topic, you should study at least three different movements as examples in at least two different regions.

Topic 9: Emergence and development of democratic states (1848–2000): Again, the word *emergence* is important in this topic, as it "focuses on exploring the post-1848 emergence of democratic states". For a state to serve as an appropriate example, therefore, it needs to have emerged within the time limits of the topic. This restriction excludes the United States, for example. Although it did *develop* as a democratic state during this period, it emerged as a democratic state before this period. Again, you should prepare at least three different states, at least two of which are from different regions.

Topic 10: Authoritarian states (20th century): The first aspect of this topic to note when determining appropriate examples is the word *states*. Although leaders are an important part of the content for this topic, and a number of 20th-century authoritarian states had but one leader (Nazi Germany, for example), the focus should be on the *state as a whole*. Again, the word *emergence* becomes significant here. Consider the following question:

> To what extent did economic factors contribute to the emergence of two authoritarian states, each from a different region?

While using the USSR is appropriate, the emergence of Stalinist Russia would not be, as Stalin came to power *after* the emergence of the state itself. You should prepare at least three different states, at least two of which are from different regions.

Topic 11: Causes and effects of 20th-century wars: There are several things to keep in mind when preparing examples for this topic. The topic indicates that you need to understand different types of wars, specifically civil wars, wars between states, and guerrilla wars. Further, you need to choose wars from at least two different regions. This means you need to prepare up to six wars – two civil wars, two wars between states, and two guerilla wars. Fortunately, you can be efficient as some wars can be used as examples of more than one type of war. For example, the Vietnam War from 1954 to1975 can be used both as a civil war and a guerrilla war. This does not apply to all civil wars, however. The Spanish Civil War did not have a significant guerrilla component to it.

You can also use the First and Second World Wars as *cross regional* wars. This means that you can use the Second World War in the Pacific as a war and, if a second war is required, you could use a European war so long as it is not the Second World War in Europe. You cannot use a cross regional war as examples of two wars in different regions in the same response. In short, you cannot compare the First World War or the Second World War to itself. One last note: the Cold War as a whole is not an appropriate example for this topic, though wars within the Cold War, such as the Korean War, could be appropriate.

Topic 12: The Cold War: Superpower tensions and rivalries (20th century): The focus of this topic is the Cold War in a global context. It requires you to prepare material on at least two Cold War leaders from different regions, two Cold War countries from different regions, and two Cold War crises from different regions. Again, you can gain efficiencies by overlapping countries and leaders. For example, you could prepare China as a Cold War country and Mao Zedong as a Cold War leader. Remember, when discussing Cold War crises, the focus of the examples you choose needs to be on superpower tension and rivalries. This means if you choose the North Korean invasion of South Korea in 1950, the focus of your response cannot be the war, but rather the crisis caused by the invasion.

Links: Structuring a comparative response

Paper 2 questions can ask you to compare and contrast examples chosen from different regions. While there are a number of ways to structure a compare-and-contrast essay, the important thing to remember is that it needs to integrate the elements that are being compared. The most straightforward way to do this is to dedicate one paragraph to analysing the similarities and another to the differences. You can also look at themes that two elements share, and compare and contrast across these themes. For example, if you are comparing and contrasting the methods used to maintain power used by two authoritarian states, you could look at the elements that they share – propaganda, force, fear, cult of personality – and create a paragraph on each of these, examining the similarities and differences of the two leaders in each.

> **Reflection**
>
> Choose two of the paper 2 questions in section 2.2. For each of these, list the appropriate example(s) you could use to answer it based on the curriculum you are studying.

The markbands

The third dimension of the markbands assesses your use of examples in your response.

▼ Table 2.4.1 How the markbands assess examples

Marks	Examples and links/comparisons
13–15	The examples that the candidate chooses to discuss are appropriate and relevant, and are used effectively to support the analysis/ evaluation.
	The response makes effective links and/or comparisons (as appropriate to the question).
10–12	The examples that the candidate chooses to discuss are appropriate and relevant, and are used to support the analysis/ evaluation.
	The response makes effective links and/or comparisons (as appropriate to the question).
7–9	The examples that the candidate chooses to discuss are appropriate and relevant.
	The response makes links and/or comparisons (as appropriate to the question).
4–6	The candidate identifies specific examples to discuss, but these examples are vague or lack relevance.
1–3	The candidate identifies specific examples to discuss, but these examples are factually incorrect, irrelevant or vague.

Source: IB history specimen paper

> **Reflection**
>
> What are the key terms used to measure the quality of the examples and links? How could you use your own words to describe answers that fall in the low markbands? What about those at the top end of the markbands?
>
> Answers: Vague and lack relevance, as opposed to appropriate and relevant and used to support. Links and effective links.

How much detail do you need to include in your answer?

Detailed information is always better than vague or imprecise information. This detail, however, needs to be relevant to the question and the analysis. Too much detail at the expense of analysis will make your response overly descriptive or narrative. We will discuss that in the next section.

If the examples chosen are not appropriate, your response will fall in either the 1–3 or the 4–6 markband in this dimension as the examples would be irrelevant. This is also the dimension in which the detail of the examples is assessed.

Markband 10–12 describes examples that move beyond simply being relevant and begin to be consciously used to support the analysis. The links to the argument are beginning to be explicit. Making direct connections with your thesis statement can help establish this.

QUESTION PRACTICE

To what extent did economic factors contribute to the emergence of two authoritarian states, each from a different region?   [15]

SAMPLE STUDENT ANSWER

▲ Two appropriate examples.

▲ Economic conditions are the focus of the question.

▲ Command term *to what extent* is understood.

▲ Qualifier.

▲ The Great Depression in Weimar is an appropriate and relevant example.

▲ The Great Depression in Weimar example is used here to support the thesis.

▲ State direction of the economy is an appropriate example of an economic policy (although Hitler's declaration happened after he gained power).

▲ Economic condition in Yan'an example is appropriate and used here to support the thesis.

▲ Land reform is an appropriate example of an economic policy.

The emergence of two authoritarian states, one under Mao Zedong in China in 1949 and another under Adolf Hitler in Germany in 1933 were to a large part determined by economic factors. The pressing economic issues facing Germany gave Hitler a wave to ride to power, while Mao's economic policies at Yan'an captivated the support of the masses. However, economic factors alone cannot explain the rise of either dictator; ideological factors and the individual characters of the two leaders were similarly vital to their ascendance.

Both Hitler and Mao harnessed the economic crises in their respective countries to catapault themselves to power. In Weimar Germany, the Great Depression of 1929 had caused wide spread suffering with eight million Germans out of work. This compounded a long history of economic hardship under the ineffectual Weimar Republic, including the hyperinflation of 1924. The desperation of Germans allowed Hitler to promote his own name and party. Indeed Hitler promised an economic miracle; he declared that he would bring private businesses under state control, eliminate unemployment, and even grant a population struggling to afford bread, a luxury – the Volkswagon car. Thus, as structuralist historian Niall historian notes, "it is in times of economic hardship that people turn to radical parties". This is precisely what occurred in Germany. In China, Mao's use of economic policies to gain the support which pushed him to power was vital. Before the Chinese Civil War, Mao was situated in Yan'an province, from 1934 to 1944. Here he implemented a myriad of economic reforms for peasants who had been exploited by the feudal system for centuries. He organised land reform programs which gained the support of these peasants. Additionally, the greater economy thrived at Yan'an, despite much of the revenue coming from the opium trade. The perceived successes of Mao's economic policies, similar to the hope in Hitler's promises, led to large scale support for Mao during the Chinese Civil War. However, another important factor in the rise of both leaders was ideological.

Mao and Hitler harnessed ideology to rise to power. In Hitler's case, he tapped into a sense of nationalism amongst the German people. This sense of nationalism had been trampled by the Treaty of Versailles issued following the First World War. The treaty stripped Germany of much of her territory, such as the Rhineland and Alsace Lorraine, and placed the entire blame onto Germany for the war through the war guilt clause. Hitler, through propaganda posters depicting the freeing of a shackled man, promised the repudiation of the Treaty of Versailles, and thus the restoration of German national pride. This factor alone garnered him widespread national support. In the case of Mao, the soon-to-be authoritarian leader harnessed the peasants' desire for a strong sovereign China, and greater equality among the citizens. Many Marxist historians present this case, arguing that after the failed 1911 revolution, the peasants were hungry for change and Mao simply tapped into this and rode the momentum for social change into power. Both the role of ideological and economic factors represents structured reasons the two authoritarian states emerged. However, it is also key to consider the unique role of the leaders themselves.

Nazi Germany and the Peoples' Republic of China could not have come into existence without the individual leaders behind the two states.

This perspective represents the intentionalist historiographical school, in which much emphasis is placed on individuals. Hitler himself played an instrumental role in the rise of the Nazi party. After being released from prison in 1924, he reorganised the NSDAP – he created Hitler youth in 1926 and worked relentlessly to garner the support of businessmen like Alfred Hugenberg, the owner of 700 German news outlets. Additionally as Ian Kershaw explores in "the Hitler myth", he established a personality cult for himself which caused Germans to weep in his presence and lovingly grant him the

▲ Effective links between the examples made here (although evidence is not supplied).

▲ Links made between examples.

▲ Cult of personality is an appropriate example.

paternal label, Führer. Evidently, contrary to what is argued by certain historians such as AJP Taylor, Hitler was not like any other leader. His organisational abilities and personality cult were unique, and they were vitally important in his rise to power. Similarly, intentionalist historians stress the active role Mao had in his own navigation to power. Mao was one of 12 who founded the CCP in 1921, it was he who led the long march in 1934, he who rejected Soviet influence and established the peasant, rather than proletariat revolution. At Yan'an, as with Hitler, he became known as a saviour and protector of the people. Evidently, economic conditions and the ability of Mao and Hitler to promise or to prove their ability to reverse the predicaments of the time were fundamental in garnering the support of the masses. However, this economic appeal went hand-in-hand with an ideological one. Furthermore, without the specific allure and organisational abilities of the two men themselves, these two authoritarian states could not have come into being.

▲ Links are made between Mao and Hitler.

▲ Links between Mao and Hitler made again in the conclusion.

In general, the material on Mao is more relevant than that pertaining to Hitler.
This response could have achieved 9/15 marks.

2.5   ANALYSIS, PERSPECTIVES, AND CONCLUSION

You should be able to:

✔ use analysis effectively on your paper 2 response;

✔ use perspectives in your paper 2 response;

✔ understand the markbands for this dimension.

Analysis

The last of the dimensions that the paper 2 markbands assess is *analysis, perspectives, and conclusion*. It is important to note that this use of the term *analysis* refers to how well a response finds connections and relationships within the historical evidence and uses these connections and relationships to answer the question. One way to look at it is that analysis happens when you lay out historical facts and then ask and answer questions about this information – questions such as *how* and *why*. In short, this dimension assesses how well your assertions and evidence fit together in relation to the question being asked.

Understanding the difference between a narrative or descriptive answer and an analytical answer is central to doing well on paper 2.

A narrative is simply telling the story of an event. Placing elements in some form of chronological order – beginning, middle, and end. But that is where it ends. A narrative response does not go beyond dealing with *what happened*. A descriptive answer communicates the surface characteristics of a historical event. It does not explain the event and its role in the bigger question.

To move beyond simple narrative or description, you must begin to address key questions:

- Why did this happen?

- How did this happen?

- What is the connection between this event and that event?

- Who or what is responsible for this happening and why?

- How does this support my position?

One way to keep your response from being too narrative is to make explicit links to the question/thesis in each paragraph. Tell the reader exactly how the evidence in your paragraph supports your position.

Perspectives

As we have already discussed, *perspectives* is one of the six historical concepts and that these are assessed in the *knowledge and context* dimension of the markbands. So why is *perspectives* showing up here as well? Here, it is specific to historical perspectives as they relate to the analysis in the response.

At its heart, *perspectives* in the context of paper 2 refers to the fact that the interpretation or experience of an event or a period in history is different depending on who you are. For example, when Christopher Columbus made landfall in the Caribbean, the experience and what came after was very different for the people who were living there than for the Spanish. Perspectives can be broken down into the following categories:

- **Individual:** Gandhi's perspective on India's independence differed from Lord Mountbatten's; Mao Zedong's perspective on removing Soviet missiles from Cuba differed from Nikita Khrushchev's perspective.

- **Group:** Women's perspective on the effects of the First World War differed from the perspective of men; the working class's perspective on industrialization differed from the perspective of the capitalists.

- **Country:** Austria's perspective on the causes of the First World War differed from those of Germany, France, Russia, and the United Kingdom; Iran's perspective on the causes of the Iran–Iraq War would be different from Iraq's perspective.

Historiography, the study of historical writing, can be used to address perspectives. Integrating the views of historians or schools of historical thought into your analysis can strengthen your response. There are, however, some important qualifications. The first is that there is absolutely *no requirement* to use historiography to reach the highest markbands. At no place in the content for paper 2 does the subject guide mention historiography. While perspectives may be required, historiography is not. Another thing to keep in mind is that any historiography you do include must be integrated into the analysis. It cannot be the focus of the response. For example, any question on the

 Reflection

For each of the topic examples you chose in section 2.4, brainstorm potential perspectives that you could include in a response. Remember, perspectives do not have to be historiographical.

>> Assessment tip

Do not waste time memorizing quotations from historians. If you are using historiography, understand the general position of the historian or school of historical thought. This will help you integrate the material into your analysis only if it's appropriate and hopefully stop it from becoming the focus of your response.

origins of the Cold War should not focus on the Orthodox, Revisionist, and Post-Revisionist schools of thought. While they can be mentioned in support of your analysis, you are assessed on *your analysis*, not those of other historians.

Conclusion

The third key element of this dimension of the markbands is the *conclusion* of your argument. In this part of the markband, we are not referring simply to the last paragraph of your response in which you summarize what has been said. Here we are looking at the conclusion to your argument and the extent to which it is consistent with the support in the rest of the response. In other words, this is the summarized answer to the question. One way to highlight this is to restate and expand on your thesis at the end of your essay, making some direct reference to the evidence you used in the rest of the response.

The markbands

The fourth dimension of the markbands assesses your historical analysis, understanding of perspectives, and the conclusion of your argument.

▼ Table 2.5.1 How the markbands assess your analysis, perspectives, and conclusion

Marks	Analysis, perspectives, and conclusion
13–15	The response contains clear and coherent critical analysis.
	There is evaluation of different perspectives, and this evaluation is integrated effectively into the answer.
	All, or nearly all, of the main points are substantiated, and the response argues to a consistent conclusion.
10–12	The response contains critical analysis, which is mainly clear and coherent.
	There is some awareness and evaluation of different perspectives.
	Most of the main points are substantiated, and the response argues to a consistent conclusion.
7–9	The response moves beyond description to include some analysis or critical commentary, but this is not sustained.
4–6	There is some limited analysis, but the response is primarily narrative/descriptive in nature, rather than analytical.
1–3	The response contains little or no critical analysis.
	The response may consist mostly of generalizations and poorly substantiated assertions.

Source: IB history specimen paper

If your response remains mostly narrative or descriptive, it cannot move past the 4–6 markband in this dimension. If you include some analysis, but only in limited amounts in proportion to the description/narrative or in a small portion of your response, in other words "not sustained", your response could reach the 7–9 markband.

Looking at the 10–12 markband, we see the introduction of perspectives and a consistent conclusion. An "evaluation of different perspectives" should be present for a paper to reach this markband, but not necessarily explicitly throughout the response.

To reach the 13–15 markband, the response needs to be clearly analytical with good support throughout. The evaluation of perspectives into your broader argument needs to be evident though not necessarily explicit.

Some words to note in the markbands:

- *Consistent* refers to a conclusion that is not contradicted by the argument and evidence in the rest of your response.

- *Coherent* describes an argument that fits together as a whole as opposed to several disjointed parts.

- *Substantiate* means to support an argument with accurate historical facts.

- *Sustained* means that the analysis is carried out through the entire response rather than isolated in one place, the conclusion, for example.

- *Clear* describes an analysis that is not difficult to follow or make sense of.

QUESTION PRACTICE

"Confrontation rather than reconciliation ended the Cold War."
Discuss with reference to the period from 1980 to 1991.   [15]

SAMPLE STUDENT ANSWER

The ending of the Cold War in 1991, with the dissolution of the USSR, can be said to have been caused by different factors, including the confrontation of leaders, like Reagan. His hardline approach could have been said to have ended the Cold War. However, other factors have to be taken into consideration. Reagan's hardline approach, a confrontational standoffish approach, is said to have ended the cold war, according to the "Western Triumphalism" school of thought. This confrontation can be seen in how he sparked the arms race, rejuvenating it after the period of defence. This can be seen in how he increased defence spending by 53% in 1982. This was due to his increased funding of anti-communist forces, like the contras in Nicaragua, against the Soviet backed Sandinistas. His increased funding for weapons too, like the Pershing II missiles, the MX ICBM (inter-continental ballistic missiles) and the B1 and B2 strategic bomber program, and the Trident SLBM initiative, and the "Star Wars" initiative all led to the increased arms race between the two nations. Furthermore, by pressuring OPEC to increase supply of oil and deflate world prices, Reagan forced the USSR to spend beyond their means. As USSR's GDP fell due to oil being their main export, they had to rely on 30% of GDP on arms compared to US's 7% as the USSR's economy was only one sixth of the US! Hence, by encouraging the USSR to spend beyond their means in such an unsustainable way, it can be said that Reagan's confrontational stance did indeed cause the implosion of the USSR, hence ending the Cold War.

▲ Content focus of question.

▲ Answer to question with brief blueprint.

▲ Qualifier.

▲ Some awareness of different pespectives.

▲ Clear, coherent analysis.

▲ Support for analysis.

▲ Clear, coherent analysis.

▲ Clear, coherent analysis that links to the question.

▲ Clear, coherent analysis that links to the question.

▲ Support for analysis.

▲ Clear, coherent analysis linked to the question.

▲ Clear, coherent analysis linked to the question.

However, there are more limitations. One would be that after 1989, the US began to pursue a non-anti-communist policy, due to a change in leadership, and cannot really be blamed for the eventual demise of the USSR in 1991. Furthermore, it was perhaps Gorbachev and his reconciliatory attitude that ended the Cold War, instead of Reagan's confrontations. Gorbachev pursued a more diplomatic approach, withdrawing troops from Afghanistan, for example. In the nations summit too, he was the one who reached out in an effort to reduce the arms race, as seen in how he talked about the Strategic Arms Reduction Treaty (START) in the Geneva summit in 1985. This hence made Reagan to also assume a more reconciliatory stance, as seen in their signing of the Intermediate Range Nuclear Force treaty after discussions in the Reykjavik and Moscow summits, which reduced the arms race between the two countries by putting a limit on the number of strategic weapons each country could have. If the Cold War is characterized on the arms race and the tensions between the superpowers, perhaps it was reconciliatory actions that ended the Cold War, instead of confrontational ones. However, one also has to talk about the role of Gorbachev in creating internal strife.

Gorbachev enacted two policies of Glasnost and Perestroika which can be said to have led directly to the end of the Cold War, by leading to the dissolution of the USSR.

Perestroika consisted of both political and economic policies. Politically, it led to the collapse of the USSR as Gorbachev allowed communist elections in the USSR's states allowing "pro-independence" Yeltsin to win and be elected giving Yeltsin significant power. This allowed Yeltsin to undermine the USSR, eventually leading to its collapse.

Economically, it was meant to streamline businesses, to make them more efficient so loss making firms would shut down allowing USSR to be more competitive. Instead, factory owners used the new found freedom to pay workers higher wages, and opted to produce luxury goods to earn more money, resulting in a food shortage. It was also unable to solve poverty, with more than 25 million living under the poverty line. Hence, this resulted in discontent against Gorbachev, and the USSR, as seen in the 1990 coal mining strikes.

Glasnost too, meaning "openness", was meant to be constructive criticism of the party. After the Chernobyl accident when Russian lives were endangered to protect the reputation of the party elites, Gorbachev felt that he should allow for criticism, to reduce corruption, and stagnation of the party. However, the releasing of political prisoners like Andrei Sakharov, increased the amount of political dissidence. The media began reporting on social economic problems that were supressed by the CPSU, subverting Gorbachev's intention of criticising the party's power, especially under Stalin leading to the undermining of the CPSU. Other Soviet states too used Glasnost as an excuse to show their discontent, as seen in elections in states like Georgia where 99% of voters voted for independence.

Hence these two policies directly undermined the CPSU's control increasing the confrontations, which eventually split the USSR into its constituent parts.

Furthermore, the society's long term economic woes should also be considered. Under Brezhnev his exorbitant arms spending could be supported by the booming extractive industries in the early 1970s, which the USSR was heavily reliant on. However, as oil prices fell, the USSR's economy increasingly became weaker, where savings increased from 11 million roubles to 221 million roubles, reducing the size of the economy. As argued by Robert L Garthoff, it was these economic woes that prompted Gorbachev to implement his policies, to help increase the USSR's falling GDP, however it had the opposite effect, leading to the USSR's demise. Furthermore it was their woes that led Reagan to pursue his confrontational stance, weakening the Soviet economy further, hence by exploiting the economic woes and the military-industrial complex, it directly led to the "Sinatra" doctrine and the reduction of the Warsaw pact capabilities, allowing countries to eventually break away from Moscow and hence the dissolution of the USSR.

In conclusion, it was the long term economic woes that led to the collapse of the USSR, eventually ending the the Cold War. It was these woes that attracted Reagan to use a confrontational means to catalyse this collapse as well as leading to Gorbachev's policy, which was the final blow to the already weakened USSR.

▲ Clear, coherent analysis.

▲ Support for analysis.

▲ Clear, coherent analysis linked to the question.

▲ Clear, coherent analysis linked to the question.

▲ Some awareness of different perspectives.

▲ Clear, coherent analysis linked to the question.

▲ A conclusion that is consistent with the argument.

This response could have achieved 13/15 marks.

3 PAPER 3

You should be able to:

✔ understand the regional options, which is the focus of this paper;

✔ understand how the regional options link up with paper 2;

✔ understand why each of the bullet points listed within the topic should be studied;

✔ develop a clear idea about the format and structure for the paper 3 options;

✔ understand the assessment criteria for paper 3;

✔ understand what examiners look for when marking this paper;

✔ acquire a better understanding of how to answer questions for paper 3, having read through the annotated student responses.

For paper 3, there are four options to choose from:

✔ option 1: History of Africa and the Middle East

✔ option 2: History of the Americas

✔ option 3: History of Asia and Oceania

✔ option 4: History of Europe.

You can see the IB's outline map of the four regions in Figure 2.1.1 on page 32.

3.1   PAPER 3 OVERVIEW

You should be able to:

✔ demonstrate in-depth study and analysis of selected regional topics;

✔ engage with the key concepts of history: causation, consequence, continuity, change, significance, and perspectives;

✔ shape a well-rounded, evidence-based response to a question that addresses one of the key concepts.

For paper 3, the specific regional option is usually selected by the teacher, in keeping with the region where the school is located or a region of study that may be of interest to the school and/or teacher. In many cases, it can and does build on what you might have studied in papers 1 and 2. Topics and events such as the Cold War, the World Wars, or independence movements studied in paper 2 are referred to in these options. The overall focus of this paper is on the important developments within the chosen region, all the way up to the year 2005. From the big picture of concepts of paper 2, the focus here is the event and how it shapes the history and developments in the chosen option.

Example 1

If option 4: History of Europe is chosen, it is likely that you have studied world history topic 11: The causes and effects of wars. It is possible that the First World War was studied as an example. For paper 3, the First World War is explored in its regional context and the global context. This exploration goes beyond the causes, practices, and effects of the First World War.

For paper 3, there is a detailed focus on the background to the First World War and the domestic tensions in Europe following the war, as well as the international impact of the First World War.

- Section 13: Europe and the First World War (1871–1918) focuses on the events that led up to the start of the First World War.

- Section 14: European states in the inter-war years (1918–1939) deals with the domestic tensions in Europe following the First World War.

- Section 15: Versailles to Berlin: Diplomacy in Europe (1919–1945) deals with international political developments following the First World War.

This is to demonstrate how the same event studied in papers 1 or 2 is explored and studied in far greater detail for paper 3.

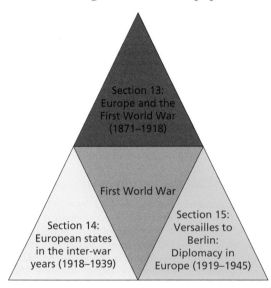

◀ Figure 3.1.1 The First World War is studied in far greater detail in paper 3

Example 2

In paper 2, you may have studied world history topic 10: Authoritarian states. It is possible that Mao Zedong of China was studied as an example of an authoritarian ruler. If you have chosen option 3: History of East Asia and Oceania, you will find that sections 12: China and Korea (1910–1950) and 14: The People's Republic of China (1949–2005) are very useful. Section 12 deals with the situation in China from 1910 to the 1950s and provides the context and background for the rise of Mao – as a member of the Communist Party, how he took over the leadership of the party in 1935 and how he came to power in 1949. Section 14 deals with Mao in power, his policies and actions till his death in 1976. The rest of the section deals with the power struggle that followed and the rise of Deng Xiaoping and beyond. Even section 9: Early modernization and imperial decline in East Asia (1860–1912) provides additional context about the situation in China up to 1912.

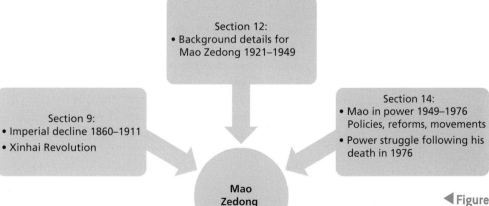

◀ Figure 3.1.2 Mao Zedong is studied in far greater detail in paper 3

"Must knows" for paper 3

For paper 3, each regional option includes within it 18 selected sections of study. The introduction at the start of each section indicates what is to be studied in the section.

Each section deals with a specific period of history within that region or a theme within the option. To explain, in option 1: History of Africa and the Middle East, section 7: The slave trade in Africa and the Middle East spans a 400-year period but the next section, section 8: European imperialism and the partition of Africa, deals with a 50-year period from 1850 to 1900.

Figure 3.1.3 is an excerpt from the IB *History guide* (for first assessment in 2020) (section on the syllabus content for HL option 2). It explains what is to be studied within a section of an option. Each bullet point breaks down the section into more manageable chunks and provides a focus for a topic of study within the section.

Note: *All* the bullet points in the section must be studied, because any of the points listed in the topic can be questioned.

14: Political developments in Latin America (1945–1980)

This section focuses on domestic and political developments in Latin America after 1945. Most Latin American countries experienced social, economic and political changes and challenges. Political responses to these forces varied from country to country—from the continuation of democracy to "populist" movements to outright conflict, revolution and the establishment of authoritarian regimes in the 1960s and 1970s. Areas of study include: conditions for the rise to power of new leaders; economic and social policies; treatment of minorities.

> This bullet point sets out why there was a revolution in Cuba.

- The Cuban Revolution: political, social and economic causes

> This bullet point refers to Fidel Castro – his rule and its impact.

- Rule of Fidel Castro: Cuban nationalism; political, economic, social and cultural policies; treatment of opposition; successes and failures; impact on the region

- Populist leaders in **two** countries; rise to power and legitimacy; ideology; social, economic and political policies; successes and failures; the treatment of opposition

> These two bullet points explore the conditions that led to the rise and rule of an authoritarian ruler – the focus could be Fidel Castro or General Pinochet of Chile.

- Democracy in crisis; political, social and economic reasons for the failure of elected leaders

- Rise of a military dictatorship in **one** country: reasons for their rise to power; economic and social policies; repression and treatment of opposition

- Guerrilla movements in **one** country: origins, rise and consequences

- Liberation theology in Latin America: origins, growth and impact

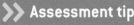 **Figure 3.1.3** Annotated excerpt from the IB *History guide*

Source: IB *History guide*

The above figure, relating to section 14 of HL option 2, demonstrates how a topic within a regional option links to and develops other topic(s) that may or may not have been studied in paper 2. It shows how region-specific topics are explored independently; the revolution in Cuba and the subsequent rise and rule of Fidel Castro, or a military dictatorship in Argentina or Chile, can be studied. This section clearly states that guerrilla movements in *one* Latin American country may be studied. There is also the option to study the rise and rule of populist leaders in *two* Latin American countries, such as Getulio Vargas of Brazil and Juan Peron of Argentina.

>> **Assessment tip**

It is important to keep in mind that only people and events referred to in the subject guide will be named in the examination questions. A copy of the subject guide will be available for your teacher, or this information may be included in any subject details that you will have been given.

Concept link

When studying for this paper and answering questions, it is necessary to remember that your course is a skilful blend of content, *concepts*, and skills. The following diagram includes the key concepts for history that should drive/shape your responses. When you read a question, you should ask yourself, which concept(s) does it address?

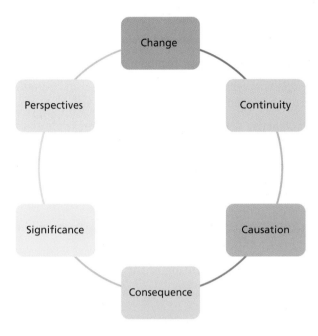

▲ Figure 3.1.4 The key concepts for history

Examples

1 Discuss the successes **and** failures of Deng Xiaoping's implementation of the Four Modernizations.

   (The concepts addressed here could include change, significance, and perspectives.)

2 Evaluate the reasons for US use of atomic weapons against Japan.

   (The concepts addressed here could be causation, significance, and perspectives.)

It is helpful to keep in mind which concepts are addressed in the question and plan the response accordingly. A good understanding of the concepts will provide a sharper focus to your response.

The assessment objectives for paper 3

The assessment objectives provide you with direction about what you are being taught and how you will be assessed. Here are the assessment objectives that are the most relevant to paper 3. Some of the key aspects of the assessment objectives have been highlighted, to place stress upon what examiners are looking for, and to provide some tips for how to prepare for this paper.

Assessment objective 1: Knowledge and understanding

- Demonstrate *detailed, relevant and accurate* historical knowledge.

- Demonstrate understanding of *historical concepts and context*.

Assessment objective 2: Application and analysis

- Formulate *clear and coherent arguments*.

- Use relevant historical knowledge to effectively support analysis.

Assessment objective 3: Synthesis and evaluation

- *Integrate evidence and analysis* to produce a coherent response.

- *Evaluate different perspectives* on historical issues and events and *integrate this evaluation effectively* into a response.

Assessment objective 4: Use and application of appropriate skills

- Structure and *develop focused essays that respond effectively to the demands of a question*.

Source: IB *History guide (for first assessment in 2020) (section in the introduction on assessment objectives)*

Do note that any response to a question in this paper will be assessed on the following qualities:

- Knowledge and understanding of the events in question.

- Ability to shape a sound argument and provide analysis.

- Ability to evaluate different perspective on issues and events.

- Ability to shape a focused essay as a response to the question asked, referring to and effectively integrating historiography into your response.

>> Assessment tip

When preparing for examinations in this paper, it is important to keep in mind the importance of three things:

- *In-depth knowledge* of the topic studied.

- The *ability to select information* to use when constructing the response to a question.

  - For example, the question "Evaluate the impact of COMECON and the Warsaw Pact on states dominated by the Soviet Union" should *not* have a response on US–USSR tensions during the Cold War. The response should focus on the two USSR sponsored institutions and their impact on USSR dominated states in Central and Eastern Europe.

- *Use different perspectives on historical issues* to add to your argument.

  - For example, for the origins of the Cold War, the post-revisionist views are not as clear-cut as the traditional and revisionist views. For the question "Evaluate the reasons for the emergence of the Cold War by 1949", a response could look at the differing views on the origins of the Cold War.

The use of historiography is a *choice* that adds value to your writing but does not lose you marks if you don't use it. If you incorporate historiography in your response, be sure not to name drop – "Historian X says…" – and then carry on with the essay. Refer to the argument that the historian makes and demonstrate how it adds to or contradicts your argument.

The format of paper 3

- This is a 2 ½ hour long paper.
- There will be 36 questions in all.
- There will be two questions from every section.
- Each section will be identified clearly. This is to remind you of the focus of the section and the event(s) that are to be discussed, as well as the time frame of the question set.
- Each question is worth 15 marks, so the maximum mark for this paper is 45.
- For this paper, *ANY THREE questions* may be answered. Your selection of questions will depend on the sections that you have studied. There is no reason why you cannot attempt both questions within one section.

The following example shows two questions under section 14: The People's Republic of China (1949-2005), taken from the May 2018 exam paper. Now, if you have already studied this section of the syllabus, it would be perfectly sensible to select both questions 27 and 28.

> **Section 14: The People's Republic of China (1949–2005)**
>
> **27.** Evaluate the role of the Gang of Four in the Great Proletarian Cultural Revolution between 1966 and 1976.
>
> **28.** Discuss the successes **and** failures of Deng Xiaoping's implementation of the Four Modernizations.

Reading the question paper

Reading the questions correctly is the key to answering effectively. While this is true for any subject and paper, this is extremely important for this paper. Your examiners are looking for sharp, focused responses.

Therefore, it is important to read the question carefully, interpret the demands of the question, and shape your response to it. Your response is not to the topic in question, but to the question about *an aspect* of the topic. The aspect is shaped by the command terms and the key words.

Command terms and key words

The command term in the question and the key words are like the building blocks of your response. Between them, the command term and the key words in the question provide the direction and the markers to write the response.

To have a better understanding of how to read and interpret correctly the questions that can be and are asked in this paper, it is important to revisit the command terms. The list in the reflection box gives the *must-know* terms for paper 3, and these will be used to frame the questions for this paper.

Similarly, key words are very important. If the command term provides a specific direction to shape your response, the key words are the markers to map out your route, in a manner of speaking.

Here is another example from IB *History guide* (for first assessment in 2020) (see section in the syllabus content for HL option 4: History of Europe). If you have selected option 4 and studied section 8: The French Revolution and Napoleon I (1774–1815), then you should be able to answer both the questions. However, do note that there is a difference in the type of question that is being asked.

> **» Assessment tip**
>
> When studying any section in this paper, it is important to remember that the section in its entirety should be studied. **Any bullet point of a section, including its sub-sections, can be asked about in an examination.** Your response to the question should be framed:
>
> - within the context of the question
> - within the time frame referred to in the section heading.
>
> Furthermore, the specific task should be highlighted by the command term and key words that you identify in the question.

> **⟳ Reflection**
>
> What does each of these command terms mean?
>
> - Compare and contrast
> - Discuss
> - Evaluate
> - Examine
> - To what extent …

QUESTION PRACTICE

QUESTION PRACTICE

Section 8: The French Revolution and Napoleon I (1774–1815)

1 **Evaluate** the reasons for the French success in the Revolutionary Wars of 1792 to 1799.

2 **Discuss** the reasons for Napoleon's rise to political power by 1799.

>> **Assessment tip**

Do note that the use of evidence is very important when shaping an argument in any IB history paper. Your response to any question for paper 3 should always contain analysis focused on the question, be supported by detailed accurate and relevant knowledge and have a conclusion that sums up evidence and analysis with a link back to the issue in the question.

For question 1, the command term is *evaluate* – you are being asked to make an appraisal of *the reasons* for *French success* in the Revolutionary Wars. For this question, you will need to make an appraisal by weighing up the strengths and limitations of the reasons that contributed to French success. Also, the word *appraisal* in the definition of *evaluate* asks you to judge what were the most important reasons. The key words highlighted in green give you additional direction about focus of the command term. It makes it very clear that you are to appraise only a certain aspect of the French Revolutionary Wars to shape your response.

For question 2, the command term is *discuss* – you are being asked for a balanced review that looks at a range of arguments, factors, or hypotheses that contributed to Napoleon's rise to power. Here, the key words are *reasons* and *rise to power*. Therefore, any conclusions you draw from the review should be supported by evidence.

From the above examples, it should be clear that responses to both questions *require evidence* to support the arguments. However, where one appraises or makes a judgment, the other question has very different demands – it is asking for a discussion on a range of factors or arguments and then a conclusion. In any case, in any response, you need to:

• present an argument

• present evidence to defend the view

• write a conclusion to round up your line of argument.

>> **Assessment tip**

It is very easy to be too hasty and impetuous, once you take a look at the paper. You look at the selected question, identify the topic it refers to, and since you have studied it, you want to write everything you know about it. The point of the question is to test your knowledge and understanding of the *event* in question. The *command term* and the *key words* in the question provide a very specific focus – misinterpret that command term and the focus of the response is lost. Your answer may be detailed; it may contain appropriate historiography, but may lack focus. For example, as explained earlier, for question 2 in the above Question practice, a weak essay would simply discuss Napoleon as a military leader. The response would miss the point of the question. In each section, one essay highlights this – it's a common but avoidable mistake. When reading the questions, do take a good look at the command term and key words, and *then* decide if you can answer the question. If you can, then go ahead and select it.

From the examples in this section, you should be able to see that the command terms and key words have some very important functions:

• Provide the response with a framework for your analysis;

• Provide a specific direction for the arguments that you will make in the response;

- The key words support the command term by indicating the specific direction of the analysis;

- The key words act as signposts – for example, reasons for French success or Napoleon's rise to political power.

Some typical key words for an essay could include words and phrases such as:

- reasons for…

- significance of…

- role and contribution of…

- result, impact, or consequence(s) of…

- change, support, or hinder…

What words and terms such as these do is give you specific indicators as to what aspect of the question you should focus on to shape your argument.

Understanding the markbands for paper 3 (higher level)

Before we look at how the command term shapes the response, it is important that you should understand the markbands and how these are applied to a response.

Marks	Level descriptor
0	Response does not reach a standard described by the descriptors below.
1–3	There is little understanding of the demands of the question. The response is poorly structured or, where there is a recognizable essay structure, there is minimal focus on the task.
	Little knowledge is present. Where specific examples are referred to, they are factually incorrect, irrelevant or vague.
	The response contains little or no critical analysis. It may consist mostly of generalizations and poorly substantiated assertions.
4–6	The response indicates some understanding of the demands of the question. While there may be an attempt to follow a structured approach, the response lacks clarity and coherence.
	Knowledge is demonstrated but lacks accuracy and relevance. There is a superficial understanding of historical context. The answer makes use of specific examples, although these may be vague or lack relevance.
	There is some limited analysis, but the response is primarily narrative/descriptive in nature, rather than analytical.
7–9	The response indicates an understanding of the demands of the question, but these demands are only partially addressed. There is an attempt to follow a structured approach.
	Knowledge is partly accurate and relevant. Events are generally placed in their historical context. Examples used are appropriate and relevant.
	The response moves beyond description to include some analysis or critical commentary, but this is not sustained.
10–12	The demands of the question are understood and addressed. Answers are generally well structured and organized, although there may be some repetition or lack of clarity in places.
	Knowledge is mostly accurate and relevant. Events are placed in their historical context, and there is a clear understanding of historical concepts. Examples used are appropriate and relevant, and are used to support the analysis/evaluation.
	Arguments are mainly clear and coherent. There is some awareness and evaluation of different perspectives.
	The response contains critical analysis. Most of the main points are substantiated, and the response argues to a consistent conclusion.

▼ Note the choice of words to describe the response: recognizable, minimal, factually incorrect, irrelevant, vague and the most important one of all, *little or no analysis*.

▼ Responses that correspond to this level are basic – possibly there is no understanding of the question.

▼ For this markband, note the choice of descriptors: some, attempt, lack of accuracy and /or relevance about specific examples. The most important descriptor – *limited analysis – more narrative than analysis.*

▲ For this markband, note the choice of descriptors: understanding but partial, knowledge partly accurate and relevant. The most important descriptor – *some analysis but this is not sustained.*

▲ For this markband, the highlighted terms indicate that most, if not all aspects of the assessment objectives, have been met. Knowledge and understanding – mostly accurate. *Analysis is based on appropriate and relevant examples.*

▲ Note: a *consistent conclusion* is present. This is a good indicator, the demands of the question are understood and addressed.

Marks	Level descriptor
13–15	Responses are clearly focused, showing a high degree of awareness of the demands and implications of the question. Answers are well structured, balanced and effectively organized.
	Knowledge is detailed, accurate and relevant. Events are placed in their historical context, and there is a clear understanding of historical concepts. Examples used are appropriate and relevant, and are used effectively to support the analysis/evaluation.
	Arguments are clear and coherent. There is evaluation of different perspectives, and this evaluation is integrated effectively into the answer.
	The answer contains well-developed critical analysis. All, or nearly all, of the main points are substantiated, and the response argues to a reasoned conclusion.

> ▲ For this markband, note the descriptors – these point to a response that is focused, with an awareness of the implications of the question. Note the last paragraph here – *well-developed critical analysis, main points are validated using evidence and a reasoned conclusion.*

Source: IB *History guide* (for first assessment in 2020) (see section on external assessment)

▲ **Figure 3.1.6** The paper 3 markbands

The paper-specific markbands have been annotated here, to highlight what examiners are looking for when they mark your responses. It is these very criteria that guide their decisions for the marks that they award the response.

When the examiners read the response, they will check to see if you have *understood the command term and the key words*. They will understand this from the tone of the answer and your choice of words. An answer that just tells you about the topic of the question does not indicate understanding of the specific focus of the question.

Your examiners will also check for *accuracy of details* – do you know the event(s) that are being asked about? They will also check to see if you are analysing the event *or "telling the story"*. Your choice of words is looked at closely. Adjectives and descriptive words provide clues for the examiner.

Your examiners read the response to ascertain if you can *evaluate and integrate different perspectives*. They will read the response to find out how well you can integrate the historiography. Are you name dropping? Or are you trying to use the historian's argument to add a voice to your own? From all this, examiners get an insight into how well you can *synthesize and evaluate information*. Finally, the conclusion to your response adds the final touch. *A conclusion indicates your understanding* of the question, your ability to shape your response and complete the discussion.

Your IB history HL paper 3 is 2 ½ hours long. This means you have 45 minutes per question.

- Do spend 3–5 minutes per question on planning the response.

- Do use the remaining 38 or so minutes to write up your response.

- If possible, try to save 5 minutes at the end to do a quick review of *all three* responses, which is often very useful to ensure that you have not missed out any information.

>> **Assessment tip**

It is always a good idea to do a quick mind map before you write up the response to the question.

Planning a response to the question

Why plan? It helps to provide a focus on the specific demands of the question. It will help you to select the exact details that you need to answer the question. Precision, focus, and analysis should be the key elements of a good essay.

One way to plan is to draw a very quick mind map. Each of us has a different way to approach a mind map, but keeping in mind the specific command term is useful.

For example, here is a mind map for a question from option 2: History of the Americas.

Section 12: The Great Depression and the Americas (mid 1920s–1939)

"The New Deal had a greater impact on the political system than on the economic system in the United States." Discuss.

Economic Impact of the New Deal - increased govt intervention

Potlical impact of New Deal - New Democratic Party coalition which dominate exec and jud. branches of govt

Immediate short- and long-term effects

Conclusion: impact greater of economic or political system

Impact of New Deal
Discuss

◀ Figure 3.1.7 Example mind map

Focus of the question: Impact of the New Deal

Command term: *discuss*. Impact on political system: was it greater than on economic system?

Key words: impact, political system, economic system

Required: opinions/conclusions

The mind map should just be a basic collection of key points. Use abbreviations, bullet points, a quick sketch, stick figures – whatever works for you. However, do remember to draw a line through it before you hand in your paper to the examination invigilator.

Reflection

Response writing is about planning. Under examination conditions there isn't much time to plan, but a few moments spent on thinking about how to respond to the question is useful. When planning a response, a simple rule for planning out the paragraphs can come in handy.

This is the PEAS rule for paragraphs:

P – Point of information or what the paragraph is going to focus on.

E – Evidence – relevant historical detail(s) to support the point you are going to make.

A – Analysis/assessment – weave in evaluation depending on the command term of the question.

S – Summing up – a sentence to sum up what has been discussed in the paragraph is very useful.

When writing the response to the question, the first step is to write an *introduction*. A good introduction sets up the essay and gives the examiner an idea of how well you have understood the question and how you intend to answer it.

An introduction to a response should identify the *command term* referred to in the question – it sets the context and tone of the essay.

Take this example from IB history HL paper 3 option 3: History of Asia and Oceania: "Discuss the factors that helped and hindered the rise of communism in China in the 1920s."

The term *discuss* provides some indication of the "push-pull" of the question. The question asks for factors that helped *or* hindered the rise of communism. The question is not one sided but asks for a weighing up of some kind.

An introduction should also have a *thesis statement* or at least provide an indication of what will be discussed in the response. However, it is important to point out that having a thesis statement is not mandatory. What is important is that the introduction sets out the *tone* and *direction* of the response.

Looking at responses to questions and how these are marked

Now it is your turn to apply what you have learned so far. The key elements to paper 3 have been explained. The next step is to look at how the essays are marked. The next section includes essays by option. For each, there will be three essays. A general explanation, the examiner's comments, and marks awarded will be at the end of each response.

Read the responses carefully. Each of the essays highlights different aspects: what to do, or in some cases avoid, when writing a response. The focus of these marked responses is to demonstrate to you what a good and a weak response can look like. By highlighting what was correct and not, the intent is to help you to recognize common errors and demonstrate to you how those mistakes can be avoided. Understanding the assessment objectives and assessment criteria are the first steps. Planning the essay is the next, and the last step is knowing what the common mistakes are, so that you don't make them when you are writing up the response.

3.2   OPTION 1: HISTORY OF AFRICA AND THE MIDDLE EAST

Example 1

Section 8: European imperialism and the partition of Africa (1850–1900)

Evaluate the factors that facilitated German annexation of Africa.   [15]

What is this question asking for?

1   Identify the command term *evaluate* – make an appraisal by weighing up the strengths and limitations of various factors made the annexation of Africa. Identify the key words: *factors* and *annexation*.

2   Topic of discussion: factors that *facilitate* German annexation of Africa.

3   Time frame: Africa 1850–1900.

Points to note:

• This is not a general question about the Scramble for Africa.

• This is a focused question on *specific factors that assisted* the German annexation of Africa over a 50-year period.

• This is not a general discussion on the Partition of Africa; it is specific to Germany's annexations and the factors that explain it.

Possible points for discussion

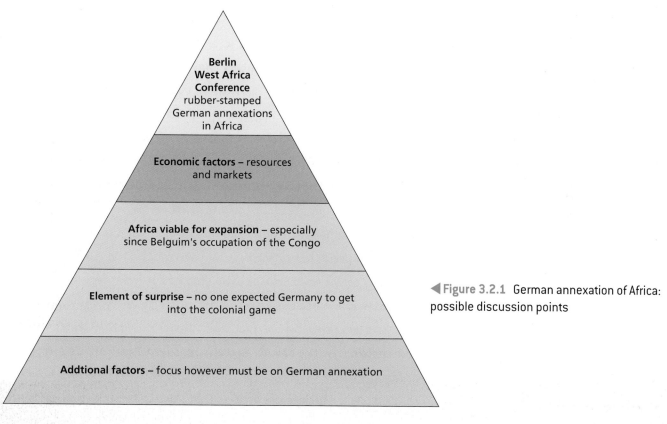

◀ Figure 3.2.1 German annexation of Africa: possible discussion points

• The significance of the Berlin West Africa Conference 1884–1885 which rubber-stamped Germany's acquisition of territories in Africa

• The role of economic factors – Africa is viewed as a potential source of raw materials and a market for finished products

• Africa seemed viable for expansion – especially after Belgium's actions in the Congo

• Element of surprise – no one had expected Germany to get into the colonial game

• General factors that explain annexation, but the focus must be predominantly on German annexation

Introduction

Germany developed as a European power after its unification (from smaller German states) in 1870. At the time the only German presence in Africa was that of German traders along the coastlines. By the time of the First World War, Germany had colonies in South West Africa, Togoland, Cameroon and Tanganyika. The interest in colonies can likely be attributed to a combination of nationalism and economic factors. The reasons for the successful acquisition of colonies were a different matter. This essay will analyse the various factors that facilitated German annexation in Africa, focusing on European rivalry, African political disunity and military weakness, technology and the role of missionaries and nationalism.

Body of the essay

Although historians such as Kiwanuka may argue that European rivalry caused rather than facilitated annexation, this is less true in the case of Germany. When Bismarck came to power as Chancellor of Germany, he did not have a great interest in colonies, choosing rather to focus on domestic issues. It may have been that he felt colonies were a waste of precious resources. It was therefore the rivalry between Britain and France in Africa that removed this obstacle – made annexation more likely and less difficult. Britain had invaded Egypt when a new power looked unlikely to protect British interests in the Suez Canal. In doing so without France, who also had a great interest in Egypt, Britain declared herself the major power in the region. This was tempered by the fact that many European states were shareholders in the canal. Britain required Bismarck's support against France and was for this reason willing to make many concessions. Mackenzie argues that Anglo-French rivalry removed any obstacles to annexation for Germany from other European powers. Britain told its government in the Cape Colony to allow Adolf Lüderitz to enter South West Africa and allow Germany huge tracts of land in East Africa. European rivalry 'facilitated' German annexation because it removed the necessity for Germany to make concessions.

There are some points to note here on the use of historiography. The student does not just name the historian, but also refers to the viewpoint put forward. The argument is further developed by referring to another historian, Gavin Mackenzie, and his view.

▼ The choice of the word "analyse" is a concern: has the student interpreted the command term correctly? Possibly the rest of the essay will provide the answer.

▲ Looking at the introduction, note that some possible factors for the German annexation of Africa are referred to. Overall the introduction sets out the context of the essay; some background detail, use of chronology is used to indicate context.

▲ Note how the student rounds off the argument in this paragraph. The student is able to make the links to German acquisitions, which is the focus of this question.

On the other hand Kiwanuka is correct in pointing out that opposition from within Europe was only one obstacle to annexation. Another was the presence of states and armies within Africa, who did not particularly wish to give up their independence. For this reason, African political weakness must be considered. Kiwanuka argues that the small sizes of the states meant that no one state could individually amass the resources to fight off the European threat. Additionally, the states were unwilling to work together to fight the European threat. Rivalries between them took precedence over fighting Europeans who many African leaders were unable to see as a threat. Furthermore Mackenzie argues that African states not only did not join together, but that they tried to use the European powers against each other. This was particularly true in South West Africa, where rivalries between the Herero and Nama were so strong that it was in fact Nama scouts that allowed the Germans to win the Battle of Waterberg and begin the Herero genocide.

African weakness must also be seen in the context of the military. The first obvious disparity must be the difference in weaponry. While Africans were still using old rifles, the Maxim machine gun had just been invented in Europe and was being put to use by Germans in gunning down Hereros from their fortresses. The significance of this technology can be seen in the fact that prior to its advent, Europeans had been afraid of the military might of the Africans. Of course, according to Mackenzie, this was not applicable to German colonizers as they had made few attempts before the technology was available. Nevertheless, it does provide evidence that without the technology, annexation would have been much more difficult. Kiwanuka supports this assessment but also argues that military weakness should also take into account strategy. Many traditional leaders were unwilling or unable to adopt new fighting strategies. In cases, where they did, such as the adoption of hit and run tactics by Witbooi's forces, and other Nama groups, they were effective in staving off the German attack. For this reason, historians have often argued that the problems (military and political) within African states must be seen as the key factor in facilitating annexation.

▲ Good linkage to the question here - there is further development of the argument from the previous paragraph. There are references to rivalry among the African states, the size of states which did not allow for the resources to deal with Europeans and also the military weakness and rivalries which blindsided the Africans to the threat of the Europeans. The student makes reference to the Herero–Nama tribal rivalry which helped German acquisition of territories in Africa.

▲ Develops the argument further by referring to the specific technology the Maxim gun and how it disadvantaged the Africans. The student clarifies their point by using relevant detail to demonstrate how the military weakness of Africans facilitated the annexation of Africa.

▼ This section refers to the additional points that explain the reasons for the German acquisition of territories in Africa, but these are generic and, at times, narrative. These points could refer to any European power. There should have been some attempt to refer to German acquisitions. Also, the use of the word "partition" is a concern, for it seems that the student is adapting from a prepared response on the Partition of Africa perhaps. Despite being generic they were nevertheless applicable to German acquisition of territory and there is a reference to the speed at which German troops could arrive, so there is a link to Germany.

▲ By linking back to Kiwanuka and Mackenzie's arguments, a link to the question is maintained.

▼ The phrase "the go-ahead" at the start of this paragraph is a little unclear. Here, the essay drifts off a little – the focus is not on the question, which is annexation by the Germans.

▲ However, the student returns to the discussion by referring to the role of traders and missionaries. Possibly this is a minor factor hence it is placed halfway through the response – as an add-on rather than a critical factor that facilitated annexation.

Technology as a factor that contributed to the success of partition must also be considered in broader terms than simply weaponry. The advent of steamships was particularly important (although perhaps not in the case of the desert South West Africa). They shortened the time it took to arrive from Germany, making it easier to call in reinforcements and to convince young men to join the colonial armies. Furthermore, they allowed penetration into the "hinterland" through rivers. Telegraphs were another invention that made the coordination of troops easier. Medical discoveries, particularly that of quinine as a prophylactic, meant West Africa was no longer "the white man's grave". It is therefore the view of historians such as Mackenzie that technology was essential in annexation, despite the fact that Kiwanuka maintains the sole importance of weaponry.

Although Germany had now received the "go-ahead" from Britain and had the power to destroy African resistance, she had no wish to do so if it could be avoided. It would be costly and reduce the possibility of using the Africans as labour. For this reason, missionaries and traders were significant in facilitating annexation. In West Africa and, to a lesser extent, East Africa trade had been strong. Germans developed links with communities that made it far easier for colonial powers to be accepted. Mackenzie in particular has argued the importance of traders, though more in relation to British colonialism. Missionaries were a second group that facilitated annexation, and an account of this is given in Olusoga and Erikhsen. When the Germans came to South West Africa, they managed to establish a colonial government that controlled part of the area (largely as a result of agreements made by the trader Adolf Lüderitz). They were not, however, able to control the Herero. When the Herero were in hiding, the colonial government used the trust they had for the missionaries to bring them out of hiding. They were then captured, and the resistance was crushed: German colonization was complete. Therefore, missionaries and traders were essential in annexation.

Overall, this paragraph seems to be more narrative and there is a sense that thread of the analysis is not clear. It does come back to the question in the last two sentences.

One final factor that can be noted was the rise of nationalism and public opinion in Germany. The wish to see a great and powerful Germany, because there was no tradition of democracy. Rather politicians avoided going against the wishes of the public so as not to cause unnecessary domestic opposition. Therefore nationalism opened the door for Bismarck to use colonies for his own political purposes.

Conclusion

There can be no one single factor that can be described as the only reason why Germany was successful in the annexation of Africa. European rivalry, nationalism, African weakness and the role of missionaries and traders all facilitated annexation because they addressed and overcame different obstacles. The metropolitan arguments would likely support the importance of European rivalry, as this was the major reason why Germany no longer feared to take actions towards colonization. However, it is probably true to say that without African political and military weakness annexation could never have happened.

▲ The response has a conclusion that sums up the key arguments.

▼ The points mentioned in the conclusion are general and lack direct links to the question that has been asked. It could be argued that this conclusion is more relevant to a general discussion on the annexation of Africa by European powers.

Overall examiner comments: Generally a sound analysis, but tighter German focus would be better – some reasons are a little generic.

This response could have achieved 12/15 marks.

This response starts off well by identifying some of the key factors that led to annexation by Germany. The first three paragraphs contained some analysis when referring to African weaknesses and the lack of African resistance to annexation by Germany. Thereafter, the response drifts to a generic discussion about technology, advances in medicine which facilitated the annexation of Africa. These points relate to any colonizing power – not just Germany. The student manages to give it a slight German focus at the end of the paragraph.

Overall, the response should focus on a critical look at factors that aided the German annexation of Africa.

The conclusion to the essay makes a judgment. "No one single factor… can be described as the only reason why…" The essay ends with another good point: "without political and military weakness, annexation could never have happened" – this is a little speculative but rounds off the response.

This response sits in the 10–12 markband. *Knowledge and understanding* is mostly accurate. *Analysis* is based on *appropriate* and *relevant* examples. Note: a *consistent conclusion* is present.

Example 2

Section 15: Developments in South Africa 1880–1994

The British won the South African War (1899–1902) but the Boers won the post-war peace. Discuss.   [15]

What is this question asking for?

1   Identify the command term: *discuss* – make an appraisal by weighing up the strengths and limitations of the argument that the Boers won the post-war peace in South Africa. Key words: *won* and *peace*

2   Topic of discussion: Developments in South Africa following the end of the Second Boer War.

3   Time frame: South Africa 1902–1949 approximately

Note: Focus is not on the Boer War but its aftermath in the context of political developments in South Africa following the Boer War.

Possible points of discussion

•   It was the Boers who would ultimately win the post-war peace.

•   The Boers surrendered and lost their independence because of the agreements concluded in the Treaty of Vereeniging (1902).

•   The difficulties experienced by the British during and after the war ensured that it was only the hollowest of victories – loss of lives and British reputation tarnished by "scorched earth tactics" and concentration camps.

•   The failure of Milner's Anglicization policies, the granting of self-government to the former Boer Republics, and the creation of the Union of South Africa led by Boer politicians.

•   Alternatively, there may be the argument that post-war reconciliation and white political and economic domination meant that both sides were "winners".

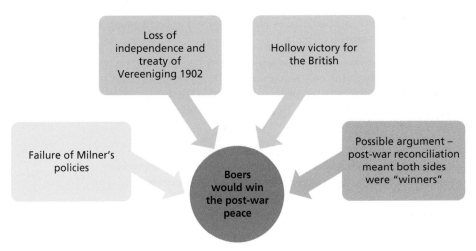

▲ Figure 3.2.2 Aftermath of the Boer War: mind map showing possible points of discussion

Introduction

The South African War that took place between 1899 and 1902 was the second war fought between two white powers of the region – the British and the Boers. The war was caused largely due to the tensions of having two powers in the region, with one (the British) employing aggressive tactics in order to benefit from the mineral wealth of the other (the Boers). The British won the war, and yet by 1910 the Boers had been given almost complete autonomy and full control over all of South Africa. The Afrikaners continued to control South Africa until 1994. For this reason, it is easy to argue that "the British won the South African war but the Boers won the post-war peace". However, there are some arguments against this statement, particularly in terms of the human cost of the war and the use of the term "won", which might be regarded as too active an explanation for many historians.

▲ The student identifies the key aspects of the essay immediately and ends the first paragraph by challenging the assumptions in the question. It brings in a third side to the discussion. Indicates an ability to look beyond the obvious, and at the implications of the question.

Body of the essay

The Treaty of Vereeniging was agreed in May 1902. Historians such as Omer-Cooper have seen this treaty as a clear indication of the Boers winning the post-war peace, as it gave an incredible number of concessions. The Boers would have to surrender, disarm and pay allegiance to the British Crown. In return for this, they would be allowed to keep their property with no land tax, and registered firearms. The Boer Republics were granted 3 million pounds in reconstruction aid, and even the allegiance to the British crown was not a huge blow to Afrikaner pride as the Transvaal and the Orange Free State were granted independence in 1906 and 1907. All of these terms placed the Boers in a strong position to begin their time as the dominant force in South Africa. Furthermore, Giliomee argues that the protection of the Afrikaner language and its adoption as primary language was particularly important as it meant the Boers had not lost any of their pride in the war and so this further developed nationalism that would develop into a major feature of the South African political landscape in future years.

A further way in which the Boers won the peace was their position in the Union government of 1910 and all the subsequent governance of South Africa. The terms of the

▲ This paragraph identifies and discusses the key argument in the essay – "Boers won the post-war peace". The paragraph sets out the argument – uses relevant and accurate details about events in South Africa following the Treaty of Vereeniging. It also refers to a historian's opinion before rounding of the discussion by referring to the development of Afrikaner nationalism. The student has selected relevant details to shape the argument.

union were such that all four areas of South Africa – the two Boer Republics as well as Natal and the Cape colony – would be amalgamated. Although under the imperialism of the British flag, the Afrikaners were in essence given autonomy in all domestic affairs and would, after a few years be given total control of the country. There are, of course, arguments against this. Denoon and Nyeko have argued that the Union government was simply a result of a lack of British interest in maintaining a presence in South Africa, although this too can be attributed to the war. Whether or not the Boers won the post-war peace, or whether it was given them, the position of superiority that they had was nevertheless the same. Furthermore, after the war, the position of the Boers as superior to the black African majority was set. From the Treaty of Vereeniging, the British had promised to leave the discussions of black rights to later. Omer-Cooper calls this a victory, because the British were forced to do so by the Boer promise that they would continue fighting if the black people were granted rights. In the South Africa Act, which created the Union, a few classes of non-whites were allowed to vote, but the majority of the population were disenfranchised.

For the following 84 years, the Boers/Afrikaners were to develop the system of apartheid. Although this is viewed by many as simply the subjugation of black people, it had economic benefits for the white and mainly Boer population. Schwartzmann and Taylor argue that white people were given protection and work based on their race. For all these reasons, it is impossible not to give credence to the idea that the Boers won the post-war peace.

Nevertheless, there are important arguments to be made against this case. Post-war peace does not necessarily cover the time up to the end of apartheid. In the immediate aftermath of the war, the Boers were in a bad position due to the human cost of the war. Although only 14,000 fighters had died (compared to 22,000 British), 26,000 civilians had been killed. The concentration camps set up for Boer women and children had a permanent effect on the physical and mental health of many. Therefore, not all Boers won the peace. Moreover, Da Silva argues that many of the concessions made by the British in the Treaty of Vereeniging were to make up for this maltreatment, and that therefore the idea of any Boers 'winning' the peace is preposterous.

Furthermore, the war did huge economic damage to farmers. The British had followed a scorched earth policy that burned down farms and destroyed crops and livestock. Despite reconstruction aid, there were many poor Afrikaner families that found it difficult to rebuild their lives. Many of these were also cases in which the family had lost the men who might have been capable of rebuilding. On the other hand, this kind of poor white farmer was helped considerably by the policies of discrimination created by the Union and later apartheid governments. The Boers were certainly in a better position than the black African majority, and probably, according to Warwick, not much worse off than before the war.

Finally, the statement that "the British won the South African war" leaves much to be considered. In technical terms, the British did win the war. This was, however at the price of 22,000 soldiers. Moreover, the treatment of civilians poisoned the atmosphere between European powers. The British then gave control of South Africa to the Boers, so one might question what the point of the war was. For this reason some historians argue that the British did not win the war.

That the British won the war also implies that the Boers lost the war. This viewpoint has, however been argued against by historians such as Peter Warwick. He argues that the Boers were in an equally strong position to the British, and that it was the black South African majority that lost the war. They fought and died for the British in the hopes of political rights, and yet these were denied. They were also put in concentration camps and their homes destroyed but they received no reconstruction aid. Warwick further argues that the refugees were repatriated instead of being helped and that they were in a much worse position than the Boers. While this argument does not necessarily negate the argument that "the British won the war" it does place it into the South African context, pointing out that the effect on the majority of the population should be considered.

▲ This student follows up the initial questioning of the proposition with further questions which demonstrate the student's understanding of the question. What is more, the historical detail about the "scorched earth policy" or reconstruction is used to support the questioning.

▲ This is the paragraph that clinches the argument. While the earlier paragraphs challenge the point raised in the question that has been asked, this paragraph takes the discussion a little further by asking, who really won the peace? It raised the question about the vast majority of Africans. What about them? What did this bring to them?

Conclusion

It is true that "the British won the South African War but the Boers won the post-war peace". The British were the victorious power, and following from this the Boers created a system in which they enjoyed a high standard of living and all their pride, while the black population around them was subjugated. Nevertheless, it is important to consider that the human cost of the war was such that not all Boers won the peace. More importantly, in the context of South Africa, the position of the black South Africans should be considered. Overall though, very few historians would argue that the Boers did not win the post-war peace

Overall examiner comments: Reflective, insightful. Well-documented and balanced analysis.

The response could have achieved 14/15 marks.

Overall, a detailed essay that looks at the impact of the South African War 1899–1902. The student demonstrates an understanding of the demands of the essay from the very start, by questioning the statement in the introduction itself.

The student's arguments are focused and demonstrate a good understanding of the historical context, which is illustrated through the apt use of examples and references to key events following the South African war. The statement "the British won the war, but the Boers won the peace" is thoroughly examined – from the perspective of the Boers, the British, and then the response brings in the argument of the African population, who lost the most (although the overall focus of the answer needs to remain on the key words *British* and *Boers*).

The student adds to the arguments by the effective use of historiography, where the historians' voices add to the student's in either accepting the proposition or questioning the statement in the question. The response is analytical – events and effective examples are used to substantiate the arguments. The student points to the disenfranchisement of the African population as the real losers.

Overall, this is a well-written response. The implications of the question are understood and addressed.

<blockquote>
» Assessment tip

When using historiography to add value to your arguments, it would be good to do what this student has done in this essay. The historian's voice is used not just to add to the student's voice but to accept the proposition or question the proposition in the question.

Use of historiography is *not compulsory,* but should you use it, allow it to add to your voice and your views or use it to challenge the implication of a question.
</blockquote>

Example 3

QUESTION PRACTICE

Section 17: Post-war developments in the Middle East (1945–2000)

To what extent were the political developments **and** economic policies of Nasser successful? [15]

What is this question asking for?

1 Identify the command term: *to what extent* – make an appraisal by weighing up the strengths and limitations of the argument that political developments under Nasser and his economic policies were successful.

2   The response should focus on the political developments and
economic policies, with appropriate evidence used support the
point of view.

This is *not* a question on Nasser's foreign policy or the wider Arab–
Israeli conflict.

Political Developments	Economic Policies
• National Liberation Rally replaced by National Union • 1962 Replaced by Arab Socialist Union • Notion of Arab Socialism • Oppression of opposition parties • Involvement with the non aligned movement	• Agrarian reforms • Land reforms • Development of public sector • Project to build a dam at Aswan

▲ **Figure 3.2.3** Notes on political developments and economic policies of Nasser

SAMPLE STUDENT ANSWER

Introduction

Gamal Abdel Nasser, the "father" of Modern Egypt who
inherited Saad Zaghlul's "crown of the peasants" instituted
radical political economic reforms characterized by bold
moves that generally aligned himself with "the downtrodden
masses" of Egypt, as he stated countless times. Politically,
Nasser was highly successful in redesigning a system of
authoritarianism rooted in revolutionary ideology and in
aligning himself with foreign powers. Economically Nasser
was less successful in implementing land redistributions
and "Arab Socialism". In both politics and economics Nasser
found his ideology largely translated into practice with some
unintended consequences.

▲ The introduction attempts to address the issues referred to in the question. It specifically refers to political developments and economic policies of Nasser. The response shows some indication that the command term is understood. The response takes the stand that economic policies were less successful.

Body of the response

When the Revolutionary Command Council of the Free
Officers' Movement wrested government control, Nasser
famously stated "Our brothers could not start their
revolution, so we started it for them". This quote characterizes
Nasser's political development of merging revolutionary
ideology with his political authoritarianism, Nasser's loosely
structured liberation rally, the only political organ served to
"bridge" the revolution to the people. Throughout his regime,
his eponymous revolution guided the development of his

▼ This paragraph makes only limited references to political development. The comment about revolutionary ideology is confusing. The focus of this paragraph is more on the *how* of the political developments under Nasser, rather than an assessment of whether it was successful or not.

▼ There is information in this paragraph which is not relevant. The references to foreign aid and funding for the Aswan Dam do not qualify as political developments. There is also information in this paragraph that does not answer the question.

▲ The parts of the paragraph that refer to the non-aligned movement are references to an international political development, and this is certainly a valid point made by the student.

▼ Much of the rest of the paragraph does not relate to the question that has been asked.

system. Nasser's one-party system flourished as the pairing or revolution vs his own leadership style accessed Egyptian nationalism and pride. For instance, Nasser famously commented that "revolution is how Egypt can see itself off its chains and rid itself of its dark past" in 1955. Unlike other authoritarian leaders, Nasser merged near constant revolution ideology with his governance, which provided satisfaction though the Arab Socialist Union (previously Liberation Rally) limited political pluralism through disallowing contentious expression.

Nasser's foreign policy was confused. In 1952 he sought the assistance off the Western IGOs like the World Bank to help finance his projects like the Aswan Dam. However, their stipulations in the form of Structural Adjustment Policies and requiring direct supervision of Egypt's economy turned Nasser off. Nasser was able to negotiate a useful degree of foreign aid from the USA. However, after the Bandung Conference Nasser publicly proclaimed Egypt's membership of the non-aligned movement. Though the US was irked by this decision, Nasser's soon to come economic policies would invite great aid from the USSR, spiking in 1955 to nearly 55 million USD in aid. Over 15,000 Soviet technicians were sent to assist Nasser, again with projects like Aswan Dam and electrifying Alexandria. Due to Cold War politics, the US withdrew all of its aid and support from the USSR but distanced Egypt from the USA. Nasser's attempt at staying non-aligned proved challenging as the USA pressured its allies to isolate Egypt. On the other hand, Nasser convinced Iraq and Syria to join his political disagreement with the Central Treaty Organization's Pact, demonstrating his strong will amongst non-aligned Arab States in resisting US influence.

When Nasser assumed control, feudal land distributions represented an enormous threat to the Egyptian peasantry. More than 80% of the peasantry owned no land and were bound to the estates owned by the rich landowners. Beginning in 1957 Nasser launched a series of Land Reform Acts that were characterized by: seizing of land from the Royal family, placing limits about land ownership exceeding 200 feddans, and reselling land to peasants with less than 5 feddans for below market prices and with generous loans. Nasser also began establishing state run cooperatives for the poorest farmers to work jointly on. These economic policies found him popularity amongst the agricultural peasantry though great resistance from the economic elite. Further, the lack of follow up infrastructure meant that many peasants were unable to work the land purchased. By 1962, the Agrarian Reform Acts had also been passed which addressed these issues. Fiscally, they increased investment and training. Monetarily, they instituted subsidies to protect farmers from foreign markets. By 1964, Nasser had successfully reformed the agricultural foundation of the Egyptian economy. Now at least 51% of peasants owned more than 10 feddans, and spillover effects like a 300% increase in primary school enrolment were noted in rural communities. The perspective of a non-Liberal economist is that Nasser stunted the development of the free market with his Stalinesque land policies. However, Nasser recognized that monopolies and feudalism made Egypt a failed market. His policies of state intervention facilitated the upliftment of millions from absolute poverty.

Wider reaching than land redistribution was Nasser's signature 'Arab Socialism'. This brand of policy was characterized by: inflation of the public sector, heavy fiscal investments, tailored socialist policy to the Arab situation, and the will to export such ideology to the Arab world. Nasser hired thousands to the public sector as workers. By the 1960s, the public sector comprised nearly 65% of Egypt's GNP. As a direct result, the number of public works such as railways and electrical plants had nearly doubled. By 1968, bread riots occurred in Cairo as some claimed the bloated public sector was slow and inefficient. However, Egyptian industries modernized greatly as the public sector financed large scale projects essential to their development. Nasser's economic policies actually increased the capacity of Egypt to trade on foreign markets, increasing their foreign reserves, while also bolstering spillover sectors like the military.

▲ These two paragraphs include relevant details about the economic policies. There is some analysis of the effects of the policies. The success of the policies, both intended and unintended are discussed. There is an also an attempt to point to a perspective, when referring to the non-Liberal economist but it has not been developed fully.

▲ From this paragraph, it is clear the student has knowledge and understanding of Nasser's policies. There is no reliance on quotes but rather use of statistics and details. There is also a link to political developments when referring to Arab Socialism. The student demonstrates a balanced use of information because this paragraph also refers to some negative aspects of the economic development.

▲ There is some more analysis here and a limited but explicit attempt to address the command term "to what extent". This paragraph attempts to build on the previous one.

Anwar Sadat's perspective would be that Nasser undermined Egypt's foreign position and that Arab Socialism had only wasted millions towards grand yet empty projects. However, Sadat failed to consider Egypt's dire need to support the common lower classes. The large public sector may have been inefficient, but its works provided roads, schools and hospitals. As Nasser said, "2 schools every 3 days!" drastically increasing enrolment by 133% and reducing public health concerns.

Conclusion

Nasser's legacy politically and economically is contentious. Many perspectives exist. Some pointing at his economic or wartime policies as singlehandedly damning or deifying his legacy. However, on balance his policies were successful in reforming Egypt's feudal land system and modernizing industry while also establishing a revolution-based authoritarianism. Nasser was limited by his inconsistent foreign policies but still found some success.

▲ A basic conclusion – rounds off the response and shows that there is some effort to address the command term.

Overall examiner comments: A little thin politically – foreign policy of little relevance here. Depth on economic policies is good.

This response could have achieved 10/15 marks.

Looking at the essay, the student is unclear about political developments and confused them with foreign policy. There was some degree of irrelevant detail. The student was focused when it came to evaluating economic developments under Nasser. There was accurate historical knowledge, use of statistics, some analysis to support the arguments. Also, there was an attempt to refer to different perspectives, but it could have been developed further. Finally, the essay argues to a consistent conclusion and this links back to the view in the introduction.

Option 1 answers: a summary

In this section, the three sample student responses will have provided you with some guidance about how to answer the questions.

The first response showed you how to include historiography into your response. The second response demonstrated how the student can successfully challenge the statement in the question. The response demonstrated how a student has a good awareness of the demands and implications of the question and deals with it. The final response is one where the student focuses more on one aspect of the question and provided incorrect and/or irrelevant details for the other aspect of the question.

3.3   OPTION 2: HISTORY OF THE AMERICAS

Example 1

QUESTION PRACTICE

Section 17: Civil rights and social movements in the Americas post-1945

Discuss the importance of US Supreme Court rulings in advancing the civil rights movement up to 1980.   [15]

What is this question asking for?

1   Identify the command term: *discuss* – make an appraisal by weighing up the strengths and limitations of the argument that the US Supreme Courts were important in advancing the civil rights movement up to 1980. Key words: *importance, advancing civil rights, Supreme Court rulings*.

2   Topic of discussion: The role of the US Supreme Court in the US civil rights movement up to 1980.

3   Time frame: 1945–1980 from the end of the Second World War up to 1980.

Points to note: The response to this question should be a balanced review of the Supreme Court rulings that had an impact on the civil rights movement up to 1980.

Possible points for discussion

- The impact of the US Supreme Court rulings such as Brown v. Topeka I (1954) and II (1955), Browder v. Gayle (1956), The Heart of Atlanta Motel v. United States (1964), Swann v. Mecklenburg (1971), and California v. Bakke (1978).

- Also, it is possible to refer to Plessy v. Ferguson (1896), which legalized discrimination, even though it is pre-1945, as an impetus for the civil rights movement.

- While it can be argued that some rulings of the Supreme Court advanced the movement, others hindered it.

- A discussion about other rulings that affected minority groups beyond African Americans.

Here is an excerpt from the student essay itself to demonstrate how to write up a simple yet effective plan. This is just a numbered list, but it will do the job.

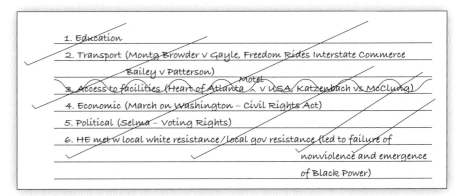

1. Education
2. Transport (Montg Browder v Gayle, Freedom Rides Interstate Commerce Bailey v Patterson)
3. Access to facilities (Heart of Atlanta Motel v USA, Katzenbach vs McClung)
4. Economic (March on Washington – Civil Rights Act)
5. Political (Selma – Voting Rights)
6. HE met w local white resistance/Local gov resistance (led to failure of nonviolence and emergence of Black Power)

▲ **Figure 3.3.1** Student's essay plan

SAMPLE STUDENT ANSWER

▲ This response is off to a good start, for it tackles the question straightaway and takes the position that the Supreme Court rulings were more significant. The basis for the discussion is indicated by referring to the Plessy v Ferguson case of 1896. The response demonstrates clearly that the command term is understood because the counterpoint is also referred to – the role of White resistance that hampered the advancement of civil rights of the African Americans. The introduction presents a road map for how the question will addressed and indicates that the limitations of the argument will also be considered.

Introduction

The US Supreme Court rulings were more significant in advancing the civil rights movement, as the Plessy v Ferguson "separate but equal" doctrine was challenged in education, transportation, and access to facilities. The US Supreme Court rulings were important in progressing and advancing the civil rights of African Americans socially, economically and politically. However, these Supreme Court rulings were met and faced with local white resistance, especially in education which ultimately became an obstacle in advancing the civil rights of African Americans, creating a sense of disillusionment regarding what nonviolence achieves. Therefore, many turned more militant as Black Power emerged.

Body of the response

Firstly, the US Supreme Court was successful in challenging the "separate but equal" doctrine in education, leading to the desegregation of education. The Brown v Board of Education case in 1955 challenged the constitutionality of the "separate but equal" doctrines. Earl Warren declared the constitutionality of the desegregation of all schools, as it generated a sense of inferiority for black children and restricted black children from an adequate education, or for every $1 spent on a white child, only 24 cents was allotted for a black child. However, Earl Warren's call for desegregation was met with both local government and white resistance, preventing its implementation. For instance, the Little Rock Care in 1957 allowed for 9 black students to go to an all-white school, however, Governor Faubus ordered the National Guard to block their entry into the school, demonstrating how local governments rejected the Brown v Board of Education rulings. Due to Eisenhower's pressures from the USSR in the climate of the Cold War as he was pressured to uphold democratic institutions for all, he called on 1200 paratroopers to escort the children. The Cooper v Aaron case in 1958 demonstrates the local white resistance, as it declared that community violence could not delay desegregation efforts. Thus, the Alexander v Holmes County case in 1969 ordered for the immediate desegregation of schools, 15 years after the Brown v Board of Education case due to white resistance and local government inactivity preventing the implementation of desegregation. Desegregation efforts still had not been fully achieved by 1960, as the Milliken Case in 1977 ordered Michigan to devise a plan to address the educational deficits for African American children and lack of desegregation efforts. This demonstrates that US Supreme Court rulings were significant in challenging the "separate but equal" doctrine in education, calling for desegregation of schools and also were important in addressing delays in desegregation.

Furthermore, the US Supreme Court was also significant in challenging segregation in public transport. The Montgomery Bus Boycott in 1956 which boycotted Montgomery Bus Company depriving them of their income resulted in the Browder v Gayle case. This called for desegregation of buses in Montgomery and desegregation of bus stations, demonstrating how a US Supreme Court decision led to desegregation in public transport. Further, the Freedom Rides in 1961, in which 13 volunteers travelled deep into the south ignoring segregated seating provoked resistance from white extremists, resulting in the hospitalization of many of the riders. In the face of bad publicity, Kennedy was forced to use the first show of federal

▲ Well argued. Clear knowledge shown. From this paragraph, it is evident that the student has a good understanding of the context of the question. The response demonstrates a good balance between events, their explanation and their significance in the context of advances to the civil rights movement.

▲ This paragraph contains several key points and these are very well presented enabling the student to develop the argument. The concluding sentence of the paragraph rounds off the discussion – in this case it is how the Supreme Court ruling led to the desegregation of transport.

force since Little Rock, and this resulted in the enacting of the Interstate Commerce Commission demanding the desegregation of interstate public transport as a result. Thus, the Bailey v Patterson case, 1970, resulted in the desegregation of all interstate and intrastate transportation thus demonstrating how US Supreme Court rulings were successful in provoking desegregation of transport to progress the civil rights of African Americans.

▲ Good point.

The US Supreme Court rulings were also significant in advancing the economic rights of African Americans, but were prompted by black activism. The March on Washington 1963 was a march with 250,000 people in which ¼ were white. All lobby groups showed a united front, demanding equal rights for African Americans and maintaining pressure on the government to pass the proposed civil rights legislation. Martin Luther King gave his famous "I have a dream" speech in which he equated the exodus narrative to that of the quest of African Americans to achieve social, political rights. The March on Washington increased the impetus to pass the civil rights legislation, demonstrating

▲ Good point.

how US Supreme Court rulings were prompted by black activism and pressure from this activism for legislative reform. The Civil Rights Act of 1964 was thus introduced, which called for the end of discrimination in workforce and hiring and desegregation of schools. 88% of southern schools desegregated as a result, whilst two thirds of cities of Alabama and Mississippi desegregated. The Higher Education Act 1965 was part of this Civil Rights Act, which increased funding into poor black college and increased black attendance by 400%. The Equal Employment Opportunity Commission was also introduced which investigated cases of discrimination in hiring procedures and were allowed to sue companies engaging in discriminatory hiring. Thus, this

▲ This sentence and indeed this response demonstrate how each paragraph develops a different aspect to the argument – education, then transportation and then the role of black activism.

demonstrates that US Supreme Court ruling fundamentally advanced the civil rights movement, as it progressed economic rights for African Americans, although this was prompted by black activism.

Furthermore, the US Supreme Court was also successful in advancing the political rights for African Americans.

The Freedom Summer of 1964 increased pressure on government to pass the Voting Rights Act, as Bob Moses called for white volunteers to come to the south to teach blacks how to vote and teach them how to behave non-violently. In Selma the following year, 1965, King and other civil rights activists campaigned for the Voting Rights Act and focused on Selma as less than 1% of blacks had registered to vote here and the Registration office was open only twice every month. The bad publicity that emerged as a result of the violence that erupted from Bloody Sunday increased pressure on government to pass the Voting Rights Act in 1965. The Voting Rights Act advanced the political rights of African Americans, as it resulted in the abolishment of literary tests required to vote and gave African Americans the right to vote in federal elections. It also resulted in federal offices or authorities to monitor registrars to ensure that African Americans were not barred from voting. This demonstrates how the political rights of African Americans advanced significantly as a result of the US Supreme court rulings.

Further, the US Supreme Court rulings were faced with local white resistance, which prevented the implementation of many US Supreme Court rulings. For instance, 88% of whites advocated for self-improvement rather than government action, whilst 90% opposed the Civil Rights legislation. The passing of the Civil Rights Act and Voting Rights Act was resented by the white majority, as 52% believed Johnson was acting "too quickly". The Civil Rights legislation also had little impact and significance for the north due to this white resistance. For instance, in Chicago 1966, King organized a 700 people march to advocate for the end of discrimination in housing. King said how "I have never seen anything so hateful and hostile". Although this resulted in the passing of the Fair Housing Act 1968 which ended segregation in housing, it was met with white resistance as 70% of whites were opposed to having a black neighbor. This demonstrates how US Supreme Court rulings were unsuccessful in progressing rights for African Americans in the north, demonstrating the inability to replicate successes from the south to the north.

▲ This paragraph starts with signposting a key argument – political rights for African Americans. The closing sentence sums up the argument in the paragraph. All this serves to show how effectively the student uses relevant historical detail to craft the argument.

▲ This paragraph demonstrates clearly the student's understanding of the implications of the question. The student brings up a counter point – what worked in the South did not in the North.

Conclusion

In conclusion, the US Supreme Court was significant in advancing the civil rights movement, as it challenged the "separate but equal" doctrine in schooling and transport, and resulted in the advancement of social, economic and political rights for African Americans, although these rulings were sometimes prompted by black activism. However, the US Supreme court rulings were unsuccessful in advancing rights for African Americans in the north due to the inability to replicate the successes from the south to the north.

Overall examiner comments: Well argued, clear knowledge shown.

This response could have achieved 14/15 marks.

The planning for the response has been included (see Figure 3.3.1) to demonstrate how the student plans out the key arguments and how the response to the question will be presented. Planning like this helps to shape the arguments to be used in the response.

This response is a great example of how the student demonstrates all the key elements of a good response – and why it deserves a 14/15:

1. *A clear demonstration of detailed and accurate knowledge and understanding* of the question. Good use of chronology, demonstrating a good understanding of the context of the question.

2. *The response uses contextual examples.* US Supreme Court rulings and the events in Selma are used to support analysis and evaluation of the role of the Supreme Court's actions.

3. The student takes the response a step further, where *the different perspectives are examined.* While there are references to the role of the Supreme Court rulings, the student also focuses on the role and achievements of black activism. By doing so, the student clearly indicates that there are other factors to consider. Furthermore, this is integrated very well into the response itself.

4. The *response contains sound analysis* – the Supreme Court rulings are analysed for what they achieved and where black activism played a more significant role. By doing this, the main points are substantiated and the conclusion to the essay rounds off a well-written response.

Overall, the response showcases the student's understanding of the demands of the question.

Example 2

QUESTION PRACTICE

Section 13: The Second World War and the Americas (1933–1945)

Evaluate the reasons for US use of atomic weapons against Japan. [15]

What is this question asking for?

1   Identify the command term: *evaluate* – make an appraisal by weighing up the strengths and limitations of arguments to explain

the reasons for the US use of atomic weapons against Japan. Key words: *reasons and use of atomic weapons*.

2 Topic of discussion: The US rationale for the use of atomic weapons in 1945.

3 Time frame: 1941–1945 until the dropping of the atomic bombs in August 1945.

Points to note: The response to this question should be a critical review of the reasons that led to the US decision to use atomic weapons in the Second World War.

Possible points for discussion

• A look at the political, military, strategic, scientific, and emotional reasons for the decisions to be appraised.

• A key point to consider would be Japan's refusal to surrender and the US apprehensions that an invasion of Japan would be costly in terms of human lives lost.

• Other factors to consider could include: desire for revenge for Pearl Harbor, the cost of building the bomb, and the need to demonstrate US power to the Soviets.

A point to note: this question does not focus on the actual bombing of Hiroshima and Nagasaki, the immediate effects, or on the end of the war in the Pacific theatre.

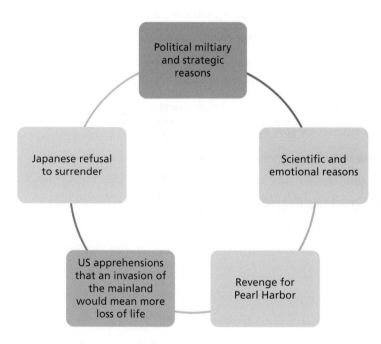

▲ Figure 3.3.2 The US rationale for using atomic weapons: discussion points

Introduction

Towards the end of WWII, Germany had surrendered, but the war still raged on in the Pacific theatre against Germany's ally Japan. The reasoning of the United States in their decision to utilize the atomic bombs was the preservation and protection of the lives of US soldiers, expediting the end of the war by striking hard and fast without giving Japan the chance to retaliate, and revenge following the attack on Pearl Harbor. While these reasons do not justify the incredible consequences of dropping the two atomic bombs for many Americans, it did succeed in forcing Japan to surrender and ending WWII in the Pacific theatre.

Body of the response

By the time that the decision was made to bomb Japan, WWII was drawing to a close with Germany surrendering and the death of Adolf Hitler. The amount of lives lost by that time was almost innumerable. One of America's goals in dropping the bombs was to save the lives of their own soldiers that could have been lost in further battle had the war continued. The remote handling of the bombing meant that no soldiers have to be actively engaging Japanese forces in order to weaken Japan on that front. This meant that the amount of American lives lost would be far less than if they had mounted an attack using soldiers on front in enemy territory.

The second justification often provided for America's actions was the desire to end WWII quickly. After the horrors that Europe in particular had suffered due to Nazi Germany and their allies and the draining of many countries' wartime resources, the world was far more than ready for the end of WWII. The dropping of the atomic bombs in Japan caused massive damage within a relatively short amount of time, instantaneously wreaking absolute destruction. This gave Japan no opportunity for defence or retaliation.

Before the attack on Pearl Harbor, the United States and mostly stayed neutral, not engaging directly in the affairs

---

▲ The response is off to a satisfactory start. Some reasons for the decision to use the bomb are stated clearly.

▼ The closing sentence of this paragraph is a cause for concern and there are indications that the response may focus more on the impact of the decision rather than the reasons for the decision to drop the bomb. The question is partially understood.

▼ The opening sentence for this paragraph could include some chronology. Also do note that it is a repetition of the first sentence in this response. There are some valid points made here, but the points lack clarity. The two sentences about minimizing loss of lives are repetitive.

▲ A short paragraph – some relevant details about why the bomb was dropped. The student could develop these specific points further. The candidate demonstrates some understanding of the question, but analysis is limited.

▼ On the other hand, there are missed opportunities for providing more details in this short paragraph, because there is more to dropping of the bomb, than just the end of the European War and the loss of life.

of WWII. After Japan attacked and bombed a military base in Hawaii, America quickly changed its mind by joining the war in retaliation. The bombings in Japan echoed the bombing of Pearl Harbor by striking quick and strong on native land. The Pearl Harbor attack had outraged American citizens and caused a call to action that eventually effected America's decision to join the war. The dropping of the atomic bombs on Japan left many Americans with little remorse and a feeling of satisfaction following the outrage of Pearl Harbor.

These reasons were not at all sufficient for the bombing of Hiroshima and Nagasaki. While Japan bombed the US, they bombed an isolated military base, costing the lives of those serving in the U.S. army and naval forces. The US bombed civilians who had no sway over the outcome of the war and spread disease in the process. The consequences of these bombings still affect Japan in the form of birth defects and genetic mutation. While the bombings did achieve the goals of ending the war in an expedient manner and saving the lives of American soldiers who may have died in combat if the war had continued, it completely disregarded the lives of innocent Japanese civilians.

Conclusion

In conclusion, the reasoning behind America's bombing of Hiroshima and Nagasaki were to save the lives of American soldiers, end the war as quickly as possible, and exact revenge for the bombing of Pearl Harbor. These reasonings in contrast to the massive loss of civilian life in Japan make the decision to bomb Japan one of the most controversial topics associated with the World Wars. While most of the world is in agreement that the Holocaust was a horrendous and completely unjustifiable tragedy, some individuals especially in America still view the atomic bombing of Hiroshima and Nagasaki as a necessary evil due to its role in bringing in WWII to an end.

Others view it as an atrocity that should have never even been considered due to the consequences and long lasting effects of the bombing. Still others remain neutral, admitting the horrific nature of the massive loss of innocent life while still supporting the bombing itself.

▼ It is this paragraph that signals or confirms the indicator in the introductory paragraph that the student may choose to focus on the impact of rather than the reasons for the dropping of the bombs. A shift away from the question is noted here and will be seen in greater detail in the next paragraph.

▼ Note here, the emphasis is on the outcome of and not the reasons for the dropping of the bomb. There is also narrative here – when there are references to bombing of civilians, which has no bearing on the question that has been posed.

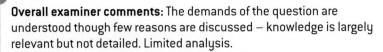

Overall examiner comments: The demands of the question are understood though few reasons are discussed – knowledge is largely relevant but not detailed. Limited analysis.

This response could have achieved 7/15 marks.

This response has been used to highlight a typical problem with question selection by students. The student has possibly misread the question and/or wandered away from the question in the response. This response also reinforces further why a quick essay plan can be helpful to provide a focus for what to write in the response.

Therefore, this response is mixed, with some valid points made at the start, but it then starts to lose focus.

Why does this response fit into the 7–9 markband? Here are the indicators for this markband:

1. *Understanding of the questions* but partial – this response starts by referring to the reasons but loses focus.

2. *Knowledge is partly accurate and relevant* – the few points referred to are accurate, but then the focus goes.

3. The most important descriptor: *some analysis but this is not sustained* – in the initial stages of the response there is some attempt to analyse the *reasons for*, but as the response of the essay focuses on the impact as well, it can be said that the analysis was not sustained.

Example 3

QUESTION PRACTICE

Section 10: Emergence of the Americas in global affairs (1880–1929)

"Wilson's policy of moral diplomacy was a failure." To what extent do you agree with this statement?   [15]

What is this question asking for?

1   Identify the command term: *to what extent* – look into the merits or otherwise of an argument, in this case Wilson's policy of moral diplomacy was a failure. There is an expectation the opinions and conclusions will be presented clearly and supported with evidence and sound arguments. Key words: *failure, moral diplomacy*.

2   Topic of discussion: Wilson's policies as president of the US.

3   Time frame: 1913–1921.

Points to note:

• This is *not* a question about Wilson and the Treaty of Versailles.

• The focused discussion should consider the merits or otherwise of the argument that Wilson's policy of moral diplomacy was a failure.

Possible points for discussion

• Moral diplomacy, both within and outside the Americas, is relevant to this question.

• The response could include the initial focus of moral diplomacy on Latin America, particularly on the Mexican government under Huerta.

- Huerta's removal could be argued a success though it ultimately led to continued civil war and Pershing's invasion of Mexico in pursuit of Villa, which failed.

- Interventions in the Dominican Republic and Haiti may also be applied as examples of failed efforts.

- The Jones Act extending more autonomy to the Philippines may be termed a success.

- Wilson's efforts to apply moral diplomacy through the Fourteen Points in the negotiations to end the First World War may be deemed a failure since the US did not join the League of Nations or sign the Versailles Treaty.

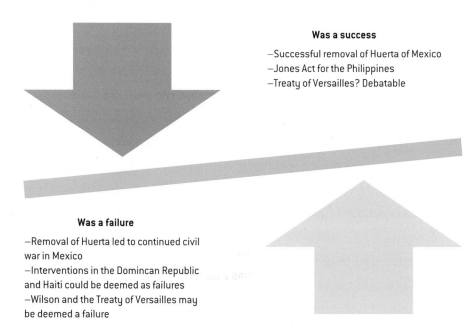

Was a success
−Successful removal of Huerta of Mexico
−Jones Act for the Philippines
−Treaty of Versailles? Debatable

Was a failure
−Removal of Huerta led to continued civil war in Mexico
−Interventions in the Domincan Republic and Haiti could be deemed as failures
−Wilson and the Treaty of Versailles may be deemed a failure

▲ Figure 3.3.3 Notes on successes and failures of Wilson's moral diplomacy

SAMPLE STUDENT ANSWER

Introduction

US President Wilson's idea of moral diplomacy in theory was to support the expansion of human rights and constitutional liberties in countries across the globe. In practice however, Wilson's diplomacy was mainly built around the ideas of supporting foreign leaders who had a similar agenda or leadership style to Wilson. Additionally, Wilson's ideas of increased human rights, freedom, and liberty seemed to not apply to colonies and occupied territories. Finally, Wilson was also unable to generate domestic support for the League of Nations, an organization whose goals of maintaining world peace and national

▲ Here is an example of a well-written introduction. The introduction spells out clearly what the discussion will be – the tone of the last sentence indicates the response will suggest that the policies were a failure.

liberties were much aligned with Wilson's domestic, moral diplomacy policies.

Body of the response

One notable implementation of moral diplomacy occurred in the middle of the Mexican Revolution. After the exile and eventual assassination of Francisco Madero, General Victoriano Huerta rose to power as the next President of Mexico. Huerta's political stance was very anti-American, which led to Wilson refusing to recognize Huerta's government. Wilson cited moral diplomacy as a justification for his actions, stating that Huerta was an abusive leader who did not attempt to offer increased human rights or liberties for the American people. Wilson attempted to endorse Venustiano Carranza as Mexico's next leader, but Carranza did not accept the endorsement.

Although Wilson did make some valid points about Huerta, his refusal to acknowledge the Mexican government meant that Huerta and his people were never able to fully operate and attempt to stabilize Mexico. Additionally Wilson's endorsement of Carranza seemed slightly hypocritical since Carranza also attacked political opposition and was anti-America like Huerto. Overall moral diplomacy failed in Mexico and contributed to several more years of instability during the Mexican Revolution.

Another issue with moral diplomacy was the fact that Wilson continually advocated for freedom and human rights in other countries but did not support civil rights for African Americans. Additionally, the US continued to control territories such as the Philippines and Puerto Rico, whose citizens were not afforded the same rights and freedoms of people in the mainland USA. Once again, this exhibited that Wilson's diplomatic philosophy was hypocritical, and this made it difficult to take seriously. Finally, in the wake of World War 1, Wilson was one of the leading representatives at the Paris Peace Conference. At Paris, Wilson presented his Fourteen Points that would assist in maintaining peace in Europe: one of the points called for the foundation of the League of Nations, an organization where each country would be represented and would work together to mediate disputes, maintain peace and advocate for human

▲ The response is off to a fine start as it addresses one of the key issues during Wilson's time in office and because the policy can be deemed both as a success and a failure. The student builds up the case for the failure of the policies and demonstrates the ability to select appropriate information to shape an argument.

▲ Good point.

▲ This paragraph maintains a critical focus on Wilson's diplomacy and highlights examples such as lack of autonomy for the Philippines or the hypocrisy of advocating human rights while not addressing the civil rights issues at home. The response also highlights Wilson's failure to garner support for the League of Nations.

rights. Essentially the goals of the League sounded like a more widescale and global version of Wilson's domestic policy of moral diplomacy. Despite this, Wilson could not gain American support for the League and the congress voted against the US joining it. The League was Wilson's brainchild and a chance for him to implement his style of diplomacy on a larger scale, but he was unable to gain support from his own country.

Conclusion

On paper, Wilson's moral diplomacy sounds extremely beneficial. Diplomacy based on advocating of human rights and constitutional liberties seems to be a very admirable way of conduct. However, Wilson's implementation of his policy was a bit more questionable. Based on his actions in Mexico, Wilson appeared to use the guide of moral diplomacy to justify becoming involved in another country's affairs, even when the alternative to Huerta did not seem much more beneficial to America. Wilson's policies can also be seen as somewhat hypocritical as he advocated for human rights abroad while African Americans lacked civil rights and American territories did not receive the same rights as the States. Finally, America's decision to not join the League of Nations was a major blow to Wilson and prevented him from implementing his policies on a global scale. Overall, moral diplomacy seemed successful in theory, but hypocrisy, questionable execution and a lack of consistency in regard to implementation greatly limited its effectiveness as a method of diplomacy.

Overall examiner comments: A sound assessment of Wilson's moral diplomacy.

This response could have achieved 12/15 marks.

The rather lengthy conclusion sums up the three key arguments that the student has used. The student has displayed an ability to select relevant historical detail, albeit some of the arguments, such as the ones about the Philippines and Puerto Rico, could have been a little more detailed.

What puts this response at the top of the 10–12 markband is the focus on the information – linking it to the issue in the question – there is analysis rather than narrative and the focus is always on the fact. The argument is that Wilson's moral diplomacy was hypocritical and not always successful. This is the point raised in the introduction and it was repeated through the essay. The essay is succinct and makes the point quite effectively, but at no time does the response question the implications of the question as does Example 1 earlier in this section.

There is limited awareness of different perspectives but this is not essential. The student has a focused argument, good analysis, and argues to a consistent conclusion.

Option 2 answers: a summary

This section deals with three responses and each highlights some interesting points about how to write effective responses.

- *Selectivity of information:* The third response in the section demonstrates how focused and relevant detail is very important.

- *The importance of reading the question and understanding its demands:* The second response here was off topic at times. The question was *reasons for* and the response was *impact of* – definitely something to avoid.

- Finally, *planning what to write:* Planning the essay pays off.

3.4   OPTION 3: HISTORY OF ASIA AND OCEANIA

Example 1

QUESTION PRACTICE

Section 12: China and Korea (1910–1950)

Discuss the factors that helped and hindered the rise of communism in China in the 1920s.   **[15]**

What is the question asking for?

1   Identify the command term: *discuss* – which means the expectation is to look at a range of factors/arguments regarding the rise of communism in China in the 1920s and come to a conclusion. Key words: *factors, rise of communism*.

2   Topic of discussion: to identify factors that helped and/or hindered the rise of communism in China.

3   Time frame: China in the 1920s.

Points to note: This is not an essay about Mao. This is a question that asks about factors relating to the growth of communism in China in the 1920s.

Possible points for discussion

- Formation of the Chinese Communist Party 1921

- Condition of the peasantry

- Sun Joffe Agreement of 1923

- Death of Sun Yixian in 1925

- The rise of Jiang Jieshi

- Mao's retreat to Jiangxi following disagreements with the CCP

- The First United Front

- The Shanghai Massacre of 1927

- The White Terror 1928

Any response to this question should focus on the 1920s from the formation of the Chinese Communist Party in 1921 to the White Terror of 1928. The extermination campaigns of Jiang Jieshi started in 1931 and are irrelevant to this question.

Therefore, where is the focus of this question? Is it an examination of the factors that contributed to, or slowed down, the rise of communism?

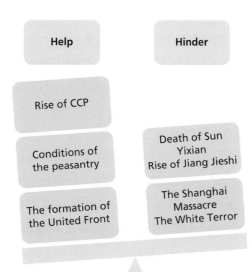

Help

Hinder

Rise of CCP

Conditions of the peasantry

Death of Sun Yixian
Rise of Jiang Jieshi

The formation of the United Front

The Shanghai Massacre
The White Terror

◀ **Figure 3.4.1** A selection of factors that helped or hindered the rise of Communism in China

SAMPLE STUDENT ANSWER

Introduction

Communism within China in the 1920s was a prominent factor with regard to the political mainframe and parties during this period. This essay aims to critically analyse and discuss the factors that helped and hindered the rise of communism in China in the 1920s with regard to the ideological changes, corruption, as well as the First United Front.

Positive: In the introduction there is some recognition that communism in China was a feature in China in the 1920s. The introduction does state an intent to analyse the factors and identifies some factors – especially a mention of the First United Front.

▼ The command term is *discuss*; however, the student uses *analyses*. It is possible the student may actually focus on the command term later on. The response states ideological changes, but this needs more clarity. Next comes the term *corruption*– of what? Of whom? Finally, there is reference to the First United Front but there is a lack of clarity here too, as no dates have been referred to. Overall, a basic attempt to analyse the question, but it fails to clarify the key aspects of the question.

Body of the essay

Firstly the GMD or Kuo Mintang were the party in power at China at the time and were led by Jiang Jieshi. 80% of China's population comprised of its peasantry hence there was a significant level of inequality in terms of distribution of wealth. The CCP however were the opposition to the GMD

▼ This first paragraph incorrectly identifies Mao as a leader at the time. There is limited reference to the conditions of the peasantry but not enough material to link the conditions to the rise of communism. Further, references to the crop yields have no relevance to the question that is asked.

▼ This information is incorrect and irrelevant. It refers to the events of the early 1930, so it is not a part of this question and cannot be used to explain the rise of communism.

▲ There is one point that is referred to. It's implicit rather than explicit – the point about lack of trained manpower. It's a hindrance to a degree.

▼ In this paragraph, much of the information is irrelevant to the question that is asked. The focus is on events in the 1930s. The student has confused the events of the White Terror 1928 with the extermination campaigns that follow later.

▼ This paragraph is poorly worded. The appeal of Maoism is not explained properly. How the CCP gained great support in the 1920s is not at all clear.

and, led by Mao, aimed to eradicate the system of wealth distribution. 92% of all land was farmland and that was the basis by which 80% of the population as peasantry gained their living as little more than subsistence farmers. During the 1920s, crop yields were significantly lower. This led to significant changes in ideology and land tax was relatively high at 25% in 1921 but lowered to a still high level of 20% in 1923. This led to distrust for the GMD among the peasantry and the substitute of communism under the rule of communism was promoted.

There were also the issues of the Japanese encroachment and the Japanese had begun to militarily seize Manchuria during this period. As such this was seen by the local Chinese population as the inability for the GMD to tackle as an issue militarily and maintain China's power internationally. This is a key factor as to why the inability of the GMD concerning the issue of Japanese encroachment led to the rise of communism in the 1920s.

Thirdly the CCP were considerably well armed and in terms of the size were much smaller compared to the GMD. They lacked the manpower to overthrow the GMD and only a minor portion of the CCP was educated to the extent required for a revolution. This is of significance to the rise of communism in the 1920s as communism possessed a lack of manpower, for the necessary reforms towards communism which acted as a hindrance.

There were five extermination campaigns carried out by the GMD against the CCP between 1926 and 1927 which further reduced their manpower and drained their resources significantly. More than 8000 of the CCP's members were either killed during the 5th extermination campaign or died before its occurrence.

The concept of Maoism as an ideology also gained mass significance in China in the 1920s as Maoism was relevant and supported but the peasantry due to its aim to eradicate the GMD and their land tax which was detrimental to the peasantry. The GMD's constant focus on the demographic of the educated upper class stimulated distrust in the peasantry, however, the CCP amassed a great support.

Furthermore, the CCP did not have any policies which catered to the benefit of the upper class and hence this may have also led to them losing support from around 20% of China's population. As such the Upper Class could further financially fund the GMD and enhance the methods of eradicating communism from the CCP within China in the 1920s.

▲ This paragraph points to a reason that the policies of the CCP did not favour the upper classes, hence a lack of support and therefore a hindrance.

Lastly the GMD did not have a very focused or united military. This was because a large number of its military army were kidnapped by the GMD and forced to serve the GMD which stimulated significant internal distrust and a lack of military unity which is of importance to the rise of communism in the 1920s as it helped the CCP gain support and weaken the GMD.

▼ Once again, we see the same lack of relevant information. The information is out of context for this question. There is reference to rise of communism but no clear reasons for what led to its rise.

Hsu stated that there was a major level of "distrust for the GMD" due to the overwhelming population of peasants and farmers which directly related to the rise of the GMD's substitute party the CCP and communism in the 1920s.

▼ There is an attempt to use historiography here, but it's too little and too late. Just a short phrase with no content to back it up. This really is name dropping more than any real attempt to use current scholarship to defend a point of view.

Conclusion

In conclusion, ideology as influenced by the growing following of Maoism and the mass peasantry support for the CCP was a key factor in the rise of communism. However, the lack of support by the Upper Class and the series of extermination campaigns by the GMD caused the rise of communism in the 1920s to be hindered.

▼ The conclusion is weak and fails to address the question. The essay referred to the United Front in the introduction, but does not mention it in the essay. There is reference to Maoism, but it is not defined. It does not focus on the reasons that led to the popularity of communism.

Overall examiner comments: A limited essay with inaccuracies and too much focus on the later period.

This response could have achieved 5/15 marks.

Points to note:

- This is a limited response as the student has misunderstood the question.

- Misreading the command term saw the focus of the essay shift to the rivalry between CCP and the GMD in the 1930s.

- Finally, there are errors in chronology.

Therefore, the real issues in the question, relating to the factors that helped or hindered the growth of communism in the 1920s in China, were not addressed.

Example 2

QUESTION PRACTICE

Section 9: Early modernization and imperial decline in East Asia (1860–1912)

To what extent did the Russo-Japanese War (1904–1905) change the balance of power in East Asia? [15]

What is the question asking for?

1   Identify the command term: *to what extent* – look into the merits or otherwise of an argument or a concept. There is an expectation the opinions and conclusions will be presented clearly and supported with evidence and sound arguments. Key words: *change* and *balance of power*.

2   Time frame: Russo-Japanese war (1904–1905), so up to 1910 or at the most 1912 as stated in the topic headline.

Points to note:

- Do remember to present both sides of the argument.

- The question asks about a possible change in the balance of power, the references should follow from the Russo-Japanese war, but the time frame should not extend beyond 1912.

- "Balance of power" refers to foreign relations/policy and the relative strength of the regional states.

Possible points for discussion

- Japan's victory and acquisition of Manchuria marked the beginning of its hegemony (dominance) of the region altering the balance of power.

- Increased Japanese influence in Korea. In 1910 Japan annexes Korea and occupies Korea until 1945.

- Impact on China should be considered, as Japan's actions had an effect on Imperial China and contributed to the Xinhai Revolution of 1911.

- Since this is a "to what extent" question, the argument could be raised that Japan had already demonstrated its dominance following the Sino-Japanese War of 1894–1895 and through the formation of the Anglo-Japanese alliance of 1902.

Victory over a European power

Acquistion of territory in Manchuria marked beginings of control in region

Increased influence over Korea

Annexation and control of Korea in 1910

Influence in Imperial China and contribution to Xinhai Revolution of 1911

Japan was already in a dominant position in East Asia by 1904–1905

Japan had achieved this position by 1894–1895 when it defeated China in the Sino-Japanese War

Japan had formed an alliance with Britain in 1902, which recognized the Japanese position in the region

▶ Figure 3.4.2 The changing balance of power in East Asia: possible points to include in your response

Introduction

The Russo-Japanese war from 1904 to 1905 was an armed conflict between the two powers in North East Asia, culminating in the victory of Japan over a western power, which was the first time an Asian power had defeated a European power in conflict. As such, Japan was able to extract several concessions such as the Liaodong peninsula and the Southern half of Sakhalin Island, whilst also decisively strengthening its influence in Korea. Thoroughly examining the effect of the Russo-Japanese war, on the role of Japan in Korea, the rise of Japanese-led Pan Asianism, as well as its repercussions on international events, this essay asserts that the war did indeed change the balance of power in East Asia to a larger extent, through decisively influencing these factors in a manner representing a significant change from previous events.

Body of the essay

It may be argued that Japanese influence in Korea had already solidified before the events of 1904 to 1905, and that Japan's victory only confirmed its dominance over the region. Since the Treaty of K/Ganghwa in 1876, where the Kuroda Mission opened up Korea's isolationism to foreign trade, Japan had remained the largest foreign community and trading partner of Korea. Its earlier victory over China in the Sino-Japanese War from 1894 to 1895, which claimed Korea as its vassal state, also allowed Japan to force China to renounce its claims and withdraw its influence from Korea in the Treaty of Shimonoseki, solidifying Japanese dominance. As such, it may be argued that Japan had already possessed a firm foothold in Korea, of which the Russo-Japanese War only served as a mere continuation of its dominance before Korea's annexation in 1910, this not representing a true shift in balance of power.

However, the role of the Russo-Japanese war in consolidating Japanese influence in Korea must not be belittled, as it enabled it to decisively engineer an international situation favourable to its later annexation of Korea. The Russian Tsar Nicholas had already expressed an eastward-looking foreign policy, intending to check the expansion of the Japanese

▲ The response makes a very good point at the start, about the first time that an Asian power had defeated a European power in conflict. This indicates that the demands of the question have been understood and will be addressed. The next two sentences confirm the student's understanding of the question. Note the use of the word *asserts* – signposts intent clearly. The last sentence refers to the command term and gives an indication of the argument that the response will make. The Russo-Japanese War did have an impact and affected the balance of power in East Asia.

▲ The student has clearly indicated in this first paragraph that the Russo-Japanese War did not mark the beginning of that shift in the balance of power. Note use of words such as *argued, confirmed* – words such as these demonstrate the ability to analyse rather than describe. Also, see the counter-argument here. This is reinforced in the next two sentences. They subtly challenge the implications of the question.

▲ This second paragraph develops the argument further by developing links to the future annexation of Korea. A historian's perspective is added to support the argument further. The closing sentence refers to the thesis in the introduction.

▲ In this paragraph the student clearly takes the discussion further – it looks at the impact of the victory on China and, at the same time, presents a counter-argument. It develops the argument, that the significance of the Russo-Japanese War as a turning point may be over-emphasized.

▲ This paragraph takes the argument yet further and demonstrates the student's mastery of the subject. The development of the idea of Pan-Asianism used by Japan to extend its influence beyond East Asia, into South East Asia too. This also demonstrates the idea that the aftermath of the war was significant for Japan. The student has pushed, subtly, the boundaries of the question.

"yellow peril" in Korea. This may be evidenced through its increasing influence over affairs in Korea, with the Korean Queen Min originally intending to pursue closer ties with Russia, as well as the Korean court temporarily ruling for a year from the Russian embassy. As such, the Russo-Japanese War allowed Japan to decisively expel its last competitor in the region. In addition, historian Michael Seth argues that the defeat of a western power legitimized Japan's claims to Korea, being seen as a rightful contender for Japanese territory, given its military prowess. Therefore this allowed Japan to annex Korea in 1910 with few objections from the international community. Thus, the war did indeed precipitate a change in the balance of power.

In addition, it may be argued that Japanese Pan-Asianism was present long before 1904, and had already permeated Japanese foreign policy to the extent that its spread after 1905 was not a true change in Japanese status on the world stage. After the Sino-Japanese war in 1895, over 20,000 Chinese students entered Japan, intending to learn from Japanese reforms to initiate Japanese-style reforms within China itself. Before this, in the 1884 Gapsin coup in Korea, the Enlightenment Party had also intended to enact Japanese-style reforms and pursue closer ties with Japan. Hence, it may be argued that Pan-Asianism was already present before the Russo-Japanese war, being exported through a common admiration for the "Japanese Way" as fostering a spirit of solidarity with other Asian nations. Hence it may be argued that this did not truly constitute a change in the international situation.

However, this may be limited with the evidence that the defeat of a Western power was crucial as it allowed for the expansion of Pan-Asianism beyond traditional Asian borders, resulting in a shift in the balance of power towards Japan. As argued by historian Selcuk Esenbel, the Russo-Japanese War precipitated the Islamic policy of Kaikyo Seisaku, resulting in an outreach towards Islamic minorities in China and Southeast Asia. Such minorities viewed the "Japanese Way" as legitimized by its show of strength against a western power, and thus a viable cultural and societal guideline applicable beyond traditional Asian ethnicities, and a truly global form of political inspiration. Hence the defeat of a western power was able to precipitate Pan-Asianism in a manner transcending typical Asian boundaries, building upon a more inclusive sentiment which expanded its influence greater than before.

Furthermore, it may be argued that the Russo-Japanese war held an undeniable influence in possessing repercussions on international events, with its future effects on East Asia and Western attitudes towards the region. The role of the war in involving Russian forces in the Asian theatre had repercussions on Russia's future ability to exert its influence on the region. As argued by historian Jon Kusber, the Russo-Japanese war was the most important factor in the Russian Revolution of 1905, as the sending of forces away from Europe reduced Russia's ability to suppress dissent at home. In addition, returning forces after the war, being disenchanted and demoralized, would participate in the events themselves. As such, this period of significant domestic turmoil would permanently shift Russia's focus away from the East Asian region, in order to consolidate its base in Europe, resulting in the permanent decline of Russian influence in Asia as a whole. Thus it may be argued that the Russo-Japanese War contributed to an international situation increasingly in Japan and favour, shifting the balance of power.

Furthermore, the events of 1905 were crucial to international attitudes towards Japan and their significant change. Before the war, western powers still possessed a low opinion of Japan, as evidenced by the Triple Intervention of Russia, France and Germany after the Sino-Japanese war, forcing them to withdraw from the concession of Liaodong it had gained from China. Events such as the 1902 Anglo-Japanese Alliance, resulting in the first military alliance between a Western and Asian power, as argued by historian Peter Duus as a pre-emptive protection against European forces such as Russia, rather than a genuine change in international opinion. However, after the Russo-Japanese War, Japan's status would rise significantly, especially through its ability to extract concessions from a Western power. This may be

▲ Here the student looks beyond the obvious – and considers the implications of the question. Here the student truly demonstrates understanding of both context and concepts. The student shows how the Russian withdrawal from the region created a power vacuum that Japan was then able to step into.

▲ It is interesting to see how the student strays beyond the time frame of 1912 to make a point about Japan's role in the Treaty of Versailles. The response just makes the point about Japanese dominance and leaves it there. The student also raises an interesting point about the significance of the Anglo-Japanese Alliance of 1902, to focus on the *to what extent* aspect of the question. The idea referred in the opening paragraphs is being developed here.

▲ What is important is the concluding sentence of this paragraph – a return to the thesis in the introduction. This clearly indicates that the response to the question is a well-constructed set of arguments that focus on the question.

evidenced through the united international action towards the annexation of Korea in 1910, and Japan's later privilege as the only Asiatic power at the presiding council of the Treaty of Versailles. Hence, the war did represent a significant change in the balance of power in East Asia, with Japan assuming even greater dominance over its interests than before, through the acquiescence of the international community.

Conclusion

In conclusion, although it may be argued that the Russo-Japanese war did not represent a significant change from previous continuities, it must be acknowledged that the war ultimately proved itself to be a pivotal change in the balance of power in East Asia.

Overall examiner comments: A detailed and thorough response that demonstrates a good understanding of the question.

This response could have achieved 14/15 marks.

A somewhat brief conclusion but the student may be forgiven for it, as the response demonstrates detailed and accurate knowledge of the question that was asked.

The body paragraphs of this response develop the key arguments very effectively and demonstrate the student's understanding of concepts such as *causation, change, continuity,* and *significance*. The student also uses historians' views to add perspective to the arguments put forward. The arguments overall are coherent, based on evidence, and there is a strong thread of critical analysis running all the way through this response. The conclusion reiterates the view referred to in the introduction. This is a balanced and well-developed response to the question.

Example 3

QUESTION PRACTICE

Section 14: The People's Republic of China (1949–2005)

Discuss the successes **and** failures of Deng Xiaoping's implementation of the Four Modernizations. [15]

What is the question asking for?

1   Identify the command term: *discuss* – make an appraisal by weighing up success and failures of Deng Xiaoping's Four Modernizations. Key words: *implementation, successes and failures.*

2   Time frame: 1978–1987

Points to note:

- Do remember to present both sides of the argument.

- This is NOT a question about the Tiananmen Square incident. The focus of this response has to be on the Four Modernizations.

Possible points for discussion

- Deng's role as paramount leader, the aims of the Four Modernizations, the changes in education and technology, the introduction of individual enterprises, the Special Economic Zones (SEZs).

- Resistance to reform, the demands for the Fifth Modernization of democracy, and internal unrest.

▲ Figure 3.4.3 The Four Modernizations: possible discussion points

SAMPLE STUDENT ANSWER

Introduction

Four Modernizations was an economic plan implemented by Deng after the failure of Hua Guofeng's Ten Year Plan in 1979. The policy sought to modernize Chinese agriculture, industry, technology and the Army. It introduced market-based policies which lead to the divisions on this topic. Marxist historians argue that it spurred inequality in China, whereas others are optimistic since China emerged as a superpower. By and large, in spite of initial set-backs, Chinese agricultural production improved at the cost of negative externalities. Furthermore, the changes in industry resulted in worse conditions for the working population in the short term. But in the long run, it has widely improved. Lastly the policy significantly improved China's balance of trade.

The change in agricultural production was largely a success and the policy also had a positive impact on the living conditions in the rural areas. To illustrate, Deng's Townships and Village Enterprises scheme allowed for creation of small businesses in the rural areas. This policy revived the local

▲ The introduction is focused on the demands of the question. There are references to the Four Modernizations – Agriculture, Army, Industry, and Technology. There is some assessment of successes and failures. The introduction also refers to the concepts – *change* and *continuity* – as well as offering two perspectives.

▲ This paragraph assesses one of the Four Modernizations and does so quite effectively. Relevant historical details are used to both evaluate the success of and shortcomings of the implementation of the Modernization. Voices of different historians are incorporated into the argument to lend weight to the view. Different perspectives are referred to. The concluding sentence links back to the question.

crops and supplied the rural sector with merit goods. By the end of the 1980s, this scheme employed 100 million people and more than 50% of the rural output came from there. The introduction of the Household Responsibility Scheme allowed for the reintroduction of private plots. The state lent the land to farmers and after they have fulfilled their quotas, they could retain the surplus and sell it. The agricultural production rose substantially as the level of undernourished fell from 23% to 10% in the first three years. Nevertheless, the agricultural production fell by 40% in 1989 since people were not motivated to care for the land, as the scheme only allowed short term contracts. Hence the government prolonged the contracts and the production started to grow. According to historian Maurice Meisner, the success of the agricultural reforms was hindered by pollution. It is true that the government did not impose any environmental measures. In the view of Carl Riskin, Deng's supporters considered this an evidence of success of the market forces. Jonathan Spence on the other hand claims that better yield could have been achieved if the privatization was greater. Given the account of historians it is fair to state that the Four Modernizations significantly improved the living condition in rural areas at significant environmental and opportunity cost. The reforms in industry were a pragmatic step that initially worsened the living conditions, but in the end substantially improved them. Deng decided to break the Iron Rice bowl which meant to cut down union powers and financial support of workers in order to create a business-friendly environment. Furthermore, he introduced tax breaks for 40,000 businesses from 50% to 33%. At first 100 million workers were underemployed. However, this environment attracted foreign investors and businesses that were however conditioned to sell their products in China. This abundance of output altogether with a growing demand for labour resulted in increased employment. Given the high tax (33%) the government still had enough money to invest in public good such as infrastructure, which improved living conditions. Marxist historian Charles Bettelheim argues that these were revisionist policies that would result in greater inequality. Deng Xiaoping would contend that 'some need to get rich first'. Even though it is true that

▲ This paragraph focuses on the modernization of industry. There is an assessment of successes, and analysis of the lack of success. Once more the student incorporates different perspectives to assess the policies. There is use of relevant data to support the arguments.

this might have created new elite, the rationale still stands – the government increased employment opportunities and GDP and slowly improved the living conditions.

China has significantly improved its Trade Balance; hence Deng's policies strengthened China on the international market. For example, China constituted Special Economic Zones that allowed four special tax concessions (only 15% in the first two years). Secondly it borrowed $45 billion from the IMF (International Monetary Fund) to improve its infrastructure and its technology to attract foreign investment. Afterwards, China started an aggressive export policy by which it created a trade surplus with the US. It can be argued that indebtedness could be a problem for China. However, by the end of (the) 20th century, China owned 16% of US debt. So even though it is fair to say that by borrowing money from the IMF, China became more dependent on the Western countries, but by owning the US debt this negative outcome of Deng's policies is mitigated. The success in exports also led to more revenue flowing into China. Therefore, Deng's performance on the international market was overall a success.

Conclusion

In summary, Four Modernizations increased agricultural and industrial output and also strengthened China's position on the international market. However more could have been achieved if China had prevented environmental pollution and greater privatization in agriculture. The main negative outcome might be the social inequality, but given the high tax incidence there were conditions for redistributive justice.

▲ Here the student demonstrates the ability to select knowledge to support a point of view. Once again there is a weighing up of the positives – trade balance, development of infrastructure, and ability to attract investment against debt to the IMF. This is a good discussion here about increase in exports and investments. The evaluation also focuses briefly on the issue of indebtedness.

▲ The conclusion links back to the question with some mention of positives and negatives.

Overall examiner comments: The student addresses the question, providing relevant and accurate detail; there is evidence of critical analysis. Defence could be developed further. The student has shown an awareness of different perspectives.

This response could have achieved 11/15 marks.

This is an interesting essay and has been included to point out something: the student has not evaluated all of Deng's modernizations. The information on education is missing and there is a very small reference to defence. As such, the response does not address all the possible points. However, this is offset by relevant and detailed analysis of what has been discussed. The changes are addressed, perspectives are referred to, and the significance of the Four Modernizations has been alluded to. This is why this response received a mark which is in the middle of the 10–12 markband.

>> **Assessment tip**

In this sample response, the student has shown a slight tendency to speculate. This is something to avoid in history. An unspoken rule is *to tell it as it is*. Use perspective but don't speculate on what might have been.

Looking at the markbands:

Knowledge and understanding – mostly accurate; refers to different perspectives – Marxist historians, a China specialist, and a US economist among them.

Analysis is based on appropriate and relevant examples – good use of data to support the arguments.

A *consistent conclusion* is present. This is a good indicator; the demands of the question are understood and addressed.

Option 3 answers: a summary

In this section three essays have been presented and each highlights some valid points that you should embrace or avoid.

1   The first response serves as an example of why you should try to avoid choosing a topic that you are *not sure about*. The student may know about Mao, but the question asks about the development of the Chinese Communist Party. As such, what the student knows is irrelevant and a low mark is given.

2   The second essay is an example of a well-argued response. The student displays mastery of the content by questioning the claim in the question, offers clear and knowledgeable arguments to support a point of view. One very important point to note is the *signposting*. This means that at the start of every paragraph it is clear what will be discussed and the last sentence completes the discussion. The conclusion is somewhat short but the body of the response is very well argued.

3   The third response points to something different. Here is a well-written, but not fully complete, response. Not all the points have been covered. However, the mitigating factor is the level of detail and the quality of analysis for what is present. So this essay sits in the middle of the 10–12 markband. There is knowledge, there is analysis, there is a conclusion – just not all aspects of the question have been covered.

3.5   OPTION 4: HISTORY OF EUROPE

Example 1

QUESTION PRACTICE

Section 15: Versailles to Berlin: Diplomacy in Europe (1919–1945)

"Italian foreign policy was inconsistent in the period between 1922 and 1940." To what extent do you agree with this statement?   [15]

What is the question asking for?

1   Identify the command term: *to what extent* – look into the merits or otherwise of an argument or a concept of the view that Mussolini's foreign policy was inconsistent. There is an expectation the opinions and conclusions will be presented clearly and supported with evidence and sound arguments. Key words: *inconsistent, foreign policy*.

2   Time frame: Italian foreign policy under Mussolini from 1922 to 1940.

Possible points for discussion

- Inconsistencies between Mussolini's goals and the methods he used to attain them.

- That Mussolini did have consistent goals – revision of the Treaty of Versailles, revival of Italian prestige, and expansion of Italian territory and influence in the Mediterranean – *but* methods to achieve them lacked consistency.

- It's also possible to analyse Mussolini's policies chronologically and argue that there was consistency in the methods till the mid 1930s. (The only exception was Corfu, where he did not use diplomacy.) From mid 1930s, Mussolini's policies became more aggressive but with some diplomacy.

- This is a *to-what-extent* question – the inconsistencies in the 1920s (Corfu) and in the 1930s (the Munich Pact and the 1939 Anglo-Italian agreement) may be considered.

Mussolini's foreign policy goals

Mussolini had clear goals which included:

Restoring Italian prestige

Revising post-war settlement

Expansion of Italian influence and territory in the Mediterranean (*mare nostrum*)

Chronological approach to the question

Policy in the 1920s and early 1930s was mostly consistent and pursued diplomatically.

- Locarno 1925
- Corfu (1924) was an exception

However, Mussolini's policy from mid 1930s becomes more aggressive.

- Abyssinia (1935) /Spain (1936) /Rome-Berlin Axis (1936)
- Mussolini joins the Second World War and enters the Balkans
- Inconsistencies in the 1930s could include
  - the Munich pact of 1938
  - attempts to sign an Anglo-Italian pact in 1939

▲ Figure 3.5.1 Approaching the Mussolini question

SAMPLE STUDENT ANSWER

Introduction

Mussolini's impressive regime in Italy between the years 1922 and 1940 did not always seem to reflect his fascist ideology in his foreign policy. Yet, European diplomacy was incredibly fragile and unpredictable in those post-war years. Mussolini's policy, although it seemed inconsistent during that time period, may have had a very central structure and plan created by Mussolini. This is what the Intentionalist school of thought suggests. In examining Mussolini's ideology in respect to several of his tactics and plans within his foreign policy,

▲ The introduction sets out the context of the essay to a degree. It identifies the time frame and also that there is a divergence of perspectives. The introduction indicates that the foreign policy actions were rooted in a consistent ideology.

▼ There are indications that the student would like to question the implications of the question but the indications here are weak.

▼ This is a weak paragraph. There is an attempt to look at perspectives, but this paragraph does not add any new information to what has already been said in the introduction.

▼ Makes some valid points – demonstrates the ability to select information and provide some analysis but it's unclear if the student wants to shape the response chronologically or refer to specific instances where there were marked inconsistencies.

▼ What is the basis for this comment about Greece? Also the comment of historians' perspectives is vague and this is something to avoid. The reference to the Great Depression and its impact on Mussolini's foreign policy is valid, but then the rest of the paragraph has vague references. The student is aware that the foreign policy is not consistent but does not have relevant detailed knowledge to offer in support of the claims made.

it is possible to suggest that although his foreign policy may have seemed inconsistent, it was grounded by a clear ideology.

Body of the essay

Fascist ideology accentuates two very important political ideas. Nationalism and Imperialism. These ideas lead on to the desire to expand. While certain historians such as AJP Taylor suggest that Mussolini had no ideas or plans, Intentionalist historians are adamant that Mussolini ruled with a Fascist end-goal and instead used political tactics to slowly work on his aims. These following events and the comparison to foreign policy allow us to critically analyse Mussolini had a clear goal within his foreign policy.

Mussolini's early policies (immediately following his rise to power), were significantly more diplomatic. However, this is likely to have been due to the fact that Mussolini gained power from a democratic government. Following his rise to power between approx. 1924 and 1926, Mussolini's foreign policy became much more aggressive, likely due to his nationalist rule. Mussolini sparked disillusionment from the Treaty of Versailles in the people of Italy which culminated in nationalist views, allowing him to use foreign policy aggressively. Yet, we see the first 10 years as rather peaceful as Mussolini was caught in a web of diplomacy-signing pacts such as the Stresa Front and the Kellogg Briand Pact only fortified this. In addition, Italy's attendance and mediation in the Munich Conference added to his air of diplomacy in the early 1930s.

Yet by the early 1930s, Mussolini had already shown a hint of aggression in the failed invasion of Greece. Historians' perspectives of why Mussolini began to strike around this time lead to the argument that to stay in power, in a time of Depression and economic collapse (battle of the Lira), Mussolini needed to continue to instil nationalism within the people. Thus, he made the calculated move of expanding and attempting to claim territories. These middle years within Mussolini's reign are crucial to suggesting that Mussolini perhaps had clear expansionist goals during his entire reign, but merely chose carefully when to apply his aggressive tactics.

Finally, the events that culminated near the end of diplomacy in Europe, the Mussolini nationalist support in the Spanish Civil War, the Abyssinian invasion and subsequent departure from the League of Nations, and the Tripartite Pact with Japan and Germany clearly revealed Mussolini's aggressive intentions. The use of gas in the Abyssinian invasion and Italy's grand commitment to the victory of Franco in the Spanish Civil war was very aggressive and brings insight into how Mussolini who was also a very good speaker and motivator used his aggressive foreign policy to reinforce his fascist rule and stay in power, with the policy of making Italy great again. His motto was: 'Conquest through War' and he liked to claim, even in his early days, 'for my part, I prefer 50,000 miles to 5 million votes'. Mussolini's aggressive aims that may have manifested well before his rule were clearly illustrated in these later years.

Conclusion

Overall, although Italian foreign policy was clearly inconsistent at surface level, from diplomatic to aggressive, Mussolini had likely planned such a development. Thus, Italy's foreign policy may have actually been headed for a consistent goal, if that had been Mussolini's ultimate plan. Regardless, historians today still debate whether Mussolini's actions were Intentionalist, or just from circumstances, structuralist. However, after analysing the consistency of Mussolini's aims and his foreign policy (and the change from democracy to fascism), there is evidence to suggest that Mussolini was a man of intention, and his foreign policies, in reflecting that, may have been much more consistent than we give him credit for.

▼ This paragraph refers to events in the 1930s and refers to the aggressive nature of the foreign policy but misses the point in the question – the policy was inconsistent. This is missing in the paragraph. Reading it you know that the policy was aggressive and why it was so, but that's not the focus.

▼ There is a conclusion, but it is confusing. The student seems to be more intent on the structuralist vs intentionalist debate. The conclusion finally states that the policy was consistent in spite of the seeming inconsistencies.

Overall examiner comments: There is understanding; demands are partially addressed. Needs more on Austria, Corfu, and alliance with Hitler.

This response could have achieved 9/15 marks.

The response reveals that this was perhaps a set piece essay on Mussolini's' foreign policy which the student has tried to modify to answer the question. Other than the error about Greece, the information presented mostly demonstrates an understanding of Mussolini's policy. But is not focused on the question, which relates to the nature of the policy.

Looking at the response as a whole, this response sits at the top of the 7–9 markband. It is noted that the information is partly accurate and relevant. The examiner has pointed out that there are missing elements. The response includes some analysis but it is not consistently developed through the response.

Example 2

Section 12: Imperial Russia, revolution and the establishment of the Soviet Union (1855–1924)

"The reforms of Alexander II were mainly aimed at preserving Russian autocracy." Discuss.   [15]

What is the question asking for?

1   Identify the command term: *discuss* – which means the expectation is to look at a range of factors/arguments regarding the reforms of Alexander II. Key words: *reforms of Alexander II, preserving autocracy*.

2   Time frame: 1855–1881.

Possible points for discussion

- The impact of the reforms of Tsar Alexander II on the peasantry and the aristocracy.

- There should be a considered and balanced review of what Alexander II expected to achieve through his reforms.

- It could be pointed out that Alexander II was a genuine liberal, influenced by western ideas and this was reflected in his attempts at reform.

- An alternative view could also be presented – Alexander II's aim was to preserve autocracy. There should be an attempt to demonstrate how the reforms preserved autocracy.

- The Emancipation Edict could be used as an example of an attempt at reduction of peasant unrest (negative aspects could also be covered).

- Likewise, the establishment of the Zemstva could be seen as a move towards liberal democracy, but as it was dominated by the nobility it could be interpreted as a move to extend central authority to the regions in Russia.

- The education reforms could be a genuine attempt at westernization and modernization – but both had limits.

- The question invites a consideration of both sides of the argument – benefit to the peasants or consolidation of autocracy.

- Judicial reforms.

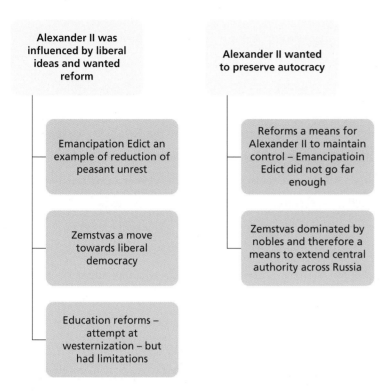

Alexander II was influenced by liberal ideas and wanted reform

- Emancipation Edict an example of reduction of peasant unrest
- Zemstvas a move towards liberal democracy
- Education reforms – attempt at westernization – but had limitations

Alexander II wanted to preserve autocracy

- Reforms a means for Alexander II to maintain control – Emancipatioin Edict did not go far enough
- Zemstvas dominated by nobles and therefore a means to extend central authority across Russia

▲ Figure 3.5.2 Approaching the Alexander II discussion

SAMPLE STUDENT ANSWER

Introduction

Alexander II, also known as the "Tsar Liberator" for his Emancipation Statute of 1861, freed 40 million serfs from their lives with no rights, a freedom owned by rich landlords, like property. With serfs making up 80% of the population, Alexander, for years was hailed as a hero, freeing the serfs and "westernizing" Russia as some historians would put it. Yet by the end of the 19th century, after many failed attempts, Tsar Alexander was assassinated, ironically on his way to creating Russia's first constitution. Since then, many historians have argued that Alexander II's motives were not humanitarian, but more out of self-preservation and the need to preserve the Russian Autocracy, that had spanned hundreds of years.

Body of the essay

Alexander's rule followed a humiliating defeat in the Crimean war, where Russia, although she had the most soldiers of any country, had one musket (long ranged rifle) for every three soldiers. This led to large casualties, poor morale and a large number of deserters. This set the basis of Alexander II's predicaments; Russia was in heavy need of industrialization

▲ The response is off to a satisfactory start but there is a tendency to be descriptive. The student refers to the key aspect of the question – the need to preserve Russian autocracy.

▼ This paragraph sets the context for the introduction of the reforms – but this is not needed. The focus of the response should be an assessment of Alexander II's motives. The student could move straight to an assessment of the impact of the reforms and question whether it was about genuine reform or an attempt to preserve the autocracy.

▲ The student makes some valid observations, which indicates an understanding of the question. The reference to reform from top down and bottom up is well made. The student presents a discussion on both sides of the question. There is some attempt to look at perspectives. The student's argument weighs in more towards preservation of the autocracy.

▼ Although the student uses the historian's voice to support the argument, the essay is moving away from the question. The paragraph reads a little like a response about the Emancipation Edict.

and reform. Thus Alexander II's following actions needed to be examined under the circumstances evoked.

The Emancipation Statute was Alexander II's single most influential reform. Yet although the nature of this reform seemed altruistic and "a step backward" for Russian autocracy, Marxist historians argued that there had to be change for industrialization and economic growth. While serfdom was agriculturally efficient, the "backwards" economy, which consisted of about 12% working class, 2% nobility, 80% serfs and the rest landlords, compared to the western powers was hugely outnumbered in workers. Thus, there came an intrinsic need to free the serfs that came from economic (and thus disillusionment and discontent from all, serfs and landowners alike, that Russia was no long a great power) need, and to preserve the autocracy. Indeed, Alexander II himself said to the nobles that they needed to create change from "top down" lest it occurred from the bottom up (revolting serfs).

A further point that supports the idea that Alexander II's reforms were mainly aimed at the autocracy was the idea that, as Orlando Figes put it "Alexander II tried to please both the autocracy and the serfs and ended up pleasing neither". This is seen through the redemption payment that he enforced on peasants – the crippling redemption payments meant that often serfs would have to work harder and for longer hours. Even though they were now liberated – often these redemption payments took about 50–60 years to pay back. Although this was very hard on the serfs, this appeased the landowners who were initially unhappy that they would have to share their land. This method meant that the serfs with no money had to buy land, and normally the land was strips, which was both impractical and useless agriculturally. Thus Alexander II's half-hearted gesture suggested that he did not indeed fully desire the emancipation of the serfs.

One of the final and arguably most significant reasons that Alexander II's reforms were aimed at preserving Russian autocracy was that he also had several reactionary reforms, aimed at appeasing the nobility, and after his assassination attempts, reforms that seemed to remove the liberty of the serfs. These included the introduction of local Zemstvas and the introduction of the Mir, both of which served different functions. The Zemstvas councils were made up of mostly landowners and nobility, which appeased them, while the Mir bound peasants to land, making sure they were unable to move around and create opportunities. Thus the result of these reforms would be agreed as reactionary – instead of further adding to his reforms and creating more liberty and democracy for the peasants, he now needed to preserve his autocratic rule.

Conclusion

Overall, although Alexander II "freed the serfs" which fundamentally seemed like a step away from the autocratic rule, many historians argue that "nothing really changed". Even industrialization did not increase enormously, as the serfs lived on Mirs, which did not let them migrate to towns and become workers. Thus, although some historians argue that Tsar Alexander II's reforms were targeted at ethical and moral compassion in liberating the serfs (as Marxist historians argue) for economic purposes – it is clear that even though the Emancipation Statute "liberated the serfs", the serfs had arguably less liberty after such liberation. Therefore it is possible to suggest that Alexander II's underlying motives for his reforms was to strengthen the Autocracy.

▲ This entire paragraph is a blend of content, context and an attempt to develop the argument further. The student uses examples such as the redemption payments and the introduction of the Zemstvas to focus on the argument that the reforms were aimed at the preservation of the autocracy.

▼ In spite of the details in the paragraph, there is a weakness, when the student refers to several reactionary reforms but leaves the discussion there, without fully developing the point.

▲ The conclusion sums up the arguments and goes back to the point raised in the introduction – reforms were introduced to strengthen the autocracy.

Overall examiner comments: Demands of the question are understood and addressed with some consideration of different perspectives. Needs to look at a greater range of reforms. Well argued.

This response could have achieved 10/15 marks.

In this response there is an effort to analyse the question by offering different perspectives. There is good understanding of the Emancipation Edict, but the response is weak when it comes to other reforms and this is obvious – there is a lack of detail. This question was based on bullet point 1 of this topic, which states: *Alexander II – the extent of reform.* This response is silent on the legal and military reforms with passing reference to reforms in education.

This response, in spite of the level of detail about the Emancipation Edict and the introduction of the Zemstvas, does not go beyond these two issues, which limits the response and therefore does not receive more than 10/15.

Example 3

Section 13: Europe and the First World War (1871–1918)

"The failure to manage the international crisis of July 1914 led to the outbreak of the First World War." To what extent do you agree with this statement?   [15]

What is the question asking for?

1   Identify the command term: *to what extent* – look into the merits or otherwise of the argument that failure to manage the international crisis of July 1914 led to the start of the Frist World War. There is an expectation the opinions and conclusions will be presented clearly and supported with evidence and sound arguments. Key words: *failure, manage, outbreak of war*.

2   Time frame: 1914, with a focus on the immediate events leading up to the start of the First World War.

Possible points for discussion

- The key crisis – the assassination of the Archduke Franz Ferdinand.

- The response to the crisis and how subsequent events led to the outbreak of the First World War.

- The July crisis should be discussed to consider the merits or otherwise of the statement that the First World War was a result of the failure to manage the crisis.

- It is possible to focus only on the events of the crisis in context, or to look at the events in the wider context and offer assessment of other factors such as militarism, imperial rivalries, and the alliance systems.

- One line of argument that could be taken is that the failure to manage the crisis escalated what was largely a Balkan crisis into a European and then world war. This argument could be taken further by arguing that previous crises such as the Moroccan crises or the Bosnia crisis had been effectively managed, and war had been averted.

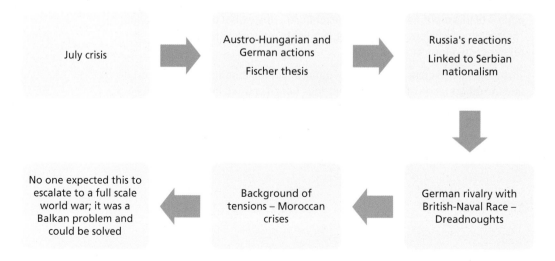

▲ Figure 3.5.3 Approaching the July crisis question

Introduction

Although the July Crisis of 1914 was the last straw which led to the outbreak of the First World War (28th July 1914–11th November 1918) the underlying tensions in Europe were already at their peak due to various factors like increased nationalism, alliance blocs, militarism and imperialism. Without these tensions, the July Crisis arguably would not have spiralled into the Great War, as with many other regional crises beforehand.

▲ The response clearly outlines the basis for discussion. The closing sentence clearly demonstrates that the demands of the question are understood. The introductory paragraph also questions the assumptions in the question. A good start to the response.

Body of the response

The July Crisis was a severe diplomatic failure for Europe, which led to the outbreak of WWI. On 28 June 1919, Gavrilo Princip, a member of the extremist Serbian nationalist group, the Black Hand, assassinated Franz Ferdinand and his wife in Bosnia. A symbol of the Austria-Hungary Empire, their citizens were outraged. The government of Austria-Hungary, however, took one whole month to respond to the crisis, a delayed response which suggests they calculated their actions.

▲ A somewhat short paragraph but it sets out the context of the discussion. The last sentence in the paragraph shows that the student intends to develop the line of reasoning. With the choice of words "took one whole month to respond", the argument is that actions were being planned rather than a knee-jerk reaction to the assassination.

In an attempt to crush rising Serbian nationalism, they requested the help of Germany, to which Kaiser Wilhelm II gives them a "blank cheque" of unconditional support, emboldening them to send a harsh ultimatum to Serbia in July. Although they had expected Serbia to reject the ultimatum, Serbia accepted all but one clause, which the Austro-Hungarian Empire still used to justify military action against Serbia. When the Austria-Hungary Empire declares war on Serbia, Russia steps in and declares war as the aggressor, escalating the conflict into the Third Balkan War. This drags Germany into the conflict to protect its ally Austria-Hungary, Germany issues an ultimatum to Russia not to interfere, another to France to guarantee their neutrality, but only received news that France would act according to its "own interns" despite King Albert's call for help, Britain did not confirm its diplomatic position on upholding Belgian neutrality as stated in the Treaty of London (only if "substantial violations" were made). Hence Germany declares war on France and marches through Belgium according to the Schlieffen Plan. Britain suddenly decides to uphold the Treaty, and the July Crisis has thus escalated from a Balkan

▲ This is a well written paragraph – given the wealth of available detail the student has been quite selective in the choice of details to construct a line of reasoning. This showcases the student's mastery of the content. Sound examples are used to support the intended argument.

crisis into an international European crisis. The European diplomats had failed to contain war.

However, it is arguable that if Germany had not issued its "blank cheque" to Austria-Hungary that the Empire would not have been emboldened and the conflict not escalated. Thus, historians like Fritz Fischer believe German nationalism was critical in the outbreak of WWI. In the Fischer thesis, Fischer stated Germany had a "will for war" given its expansionist nationalistic foreign policy – Weltpolitik. Kaiser Wilhelm II wanted to make Germany a world power like Britain. He wanted Germany to have a "place under the sun", adding to national prestige and glory, thus pursuing Weltpolitik, which antagonizes other nations as European prior balance was challenged, leading to uncertainty and heightening military tensions between nations.

To increase world power, Germany pursued alliance which could be viewed as aggressive. They had signed the Dual Alliance with Austria-Hungary Empire and later the Triple Alliance alongside Italy and the Austria-Hungary Empire. The Triple Alliance was a military alliance that guaranteed mutual mobilization for troops should one of these nations be attacked by two or more powers. This exacerbates military tensions in the region. Russia felt isolated after German failure to review the Reinsurance Treaty signed by Chancellor Otto von Bismarck before his death, which propels them to go into an alliance with France in the Franco-Soviet Alliance. To counter the Triple Alliance, this alliance was then merged with the French and British Entente Cordiale to form the Triple Entente. As such, Bismarck's web of alliances, e.g. the Drei Kaiser bund and the Triple Emperor's League, had failed under the new Kaiser, separating Europe into 2 hostile blocs. However, historian Gerhard Ritter argues that the alliances of Germany were mainly defensive to consolidate power. Germany had simply felt "encircled" which motivates her to further support her only true ally Austria-Hungary Empire e.g. July Crisis. Regardless, the alliance system split Europe into two main blocs, whereby tensions rose and a conflict may escalate to scale upon involvement of another ally.

▲ In this paragraph the student introduces another aspect of the argument – the role of Germany in the escalation of the conflict and the failure to manage it. Once again, the same selectivity of information is noted. To this is added the historian's perspective. The Fischer thesis is incorporated quite skilfully into the discussion.

▲ The information here puts the July crisis into a wider context, demonstrating the student's mastery of the content and context. The student is able to look at the immediate and into the longer-term context of the failure to manage the July crisis. The student understands that the July crisis is only a small part of the issue.

▼ One tiny error – in 1893 there was no Franco-Soviet alliance. It should be the Franco-Russian alliance. However the student is not marked down for it.

The growing militarism caused by nationalism and alliances also escalated tensions leading to WWI. First Germany was pursuing expansionist naval polities to rival British naval superiority, with the Second Naval Law doubling the German naval fleet. This scares Britain out of her "Splendid Isolation" and the two engage in a naval arms race which infamously led to the production of advanced technology like HMS Dreadnought. The other nations also responded to the growing threat of war, e.g. past Moroccan Crises, and Balkan Wars, implementing conscription and military armaments leading to a 300% increase in armaments in Europe. Furthermore, countries were beginning to create war plans. E.g. Germany with Schlieffen Plan to invade France through the less fortified Belgium, France had Plan 17 to swiftly retake Alsace Lorraine from Germany. Thus, as historian AJP Taylor argued, although countries wanted to avoid war, the escalating military tensions caused by the increased militarism and war plans left little room for other action but war.

Equally as important would be the imperialism of nations. With Weltpolitik, Germany had wanted to expand her empire. However, other European countries like Britain and France had already entered in the Scramble for Africa. Thus, French participation led to increased clash of interest which worsens diplomatic relations. For example, the Second Moroccan Crisis between France and Germany escalated into an Anglo-German conflict over Germany's aggressive demands for the whole French Congo, which is denied and worsens relations between the two alliance blocs. Germany had also sent the Kruger telegram to the President of the Transvaal Republic, causing indignation to the British and encouraged hostility towards the Germans, escalating tensions to war.

Although it may seem that German role in causing WWI is large, other nations should also be held accountable for pursuing their self-interests which led to war. German ally Austria-Hungary Empire had faced the rising Slavic nationalism with the imminent decline of the Ottoman Empire the "Sick Man of Europe", as it had many Slavs with its borders. Therefore

▲ Here too there is a continuation of the line of reasoning. This time the essay looks at the British perspective and how that may have contributed to the escalation of the existing tensions.

▲ This paragraph has an interesting twist, which once again demonstrates an understanding of the question and its implications. The student looks at German responsibility for the start of the war as well as the Russian role in the escalation of the crisis. This was followed by a quick summing up of how manage and intent converge to the outbreak of war.

it pursued an aggressive policy to contain Pan Slavism e.g. flouting the plans for Greater Serbia in the Bosnian Crisis and the First Balkan War, and most importantly the ultimatum of July 1914. But this would not have escalated into a crisis if Russia had not believed it was for the protection of Slavs and supported Serbia, mobilizing troops for them. The Russians were also emboldened by French guarantee and assistance putting France accountable too. Britain had also not declared its position during the July Crisis, which emboldened Germany. Britain was engaging in a game of low politics between Doves and Hawks, which led to war.

Conclusion

In conclusion, the failure to deal with the July Crisis was the immediate cause of the outbreak of war. However, with European countries pursuing nationalism, militarism, alliances, imperialism and self interests, tensions in Europe had already escalated to breaking points, and thus the July Crisis merely catalysed the start of WWI.

Overall examiner comments: Response is clearly focused. High degree of awareness of demands of the question. Knowledge is detailed, accurate and relevant. Well developed critical analysis. Very good on July Crisis.

This response could have achieved 15/15 marks.

This response clearly demonstrates that it is possible to attain full marks for a question. This response clearly meets all the criteria for the 13–15 markband.

The response is clearly focused on the question – that is the failure to manage the July crisis. The discussion of the immediate situation and the context of the failure clearly indicate that the implications of the question are understood. The development of the response from the introduction all the way to the conclusion – wherein each paragraph focuses on a different aspect of the argument, showcases the student's ability to structure an essay and effectively organize information.

With one small exception, information is accurate and relevant. Only the key issues that would develop the argument have been used. The argument is two-pronged – intent to escalate the crisis and the backdrop of the growing tensions have clearly been referred to. The student has skilfully woven in the Fischer thesis, the Ritter viewpoint, and AJP Taylor's arguments. All in all, the response contains well-developed critical analysis, the key points are substantiated, and the response ends with a brief but effective conclusion. Well done!

Option 4 answers: a summary

For this section too, each essay highlights key points about being prepared for the IB history HL paper 3 examinations.

1   The first response about Mussolini's foreign policy highlights how the student probably has not read the question too carefully. Either the student had a setpiece answer prepared and tried to modify that, or more likely missed the bit in the question about "inconsistent" foreign policy. This example underscores the importance of identifying and addressing the key words in a question, before you write the response to the question.

2   The second response about Alexander II's reforms points to something that should be avoided if possible. It is likely that the student was expecting a question on the Emancipation Edict and selected the question. There is a good analysis of the impact of the Emancipation Edict. However, the understanding of the other aspects of the question was limited and this is apparent in the response. It is important to study all the bullet points in a topic, for a question can be posed on any bullet point in the topic. If you have not studied and prepared for all the bullet points in that topic, then your response is likely to lack a good balance.

3   Finally, the last example is a very well written response. The level of detail is of a very high standard and the small error in chronology can be forgiven. What makes this response a truly outstanding one is the attention to detail, the focused analysis – it is a great example of how to blend content and analysis effectively. All things considered, the response focuses not just on the demands of the question, but has an awareness of the implications of the question.

Final tip: Imagine you have a bag full of information. Your command term and key words will help you pull out the relevant pieces from that bag and your essay planning will help you arrange that information effectively into a well-written and balanced response.

Reflection

Remember, you have three sets of tools to help you – each plays its own role:

- the command term
- the key words
- the key concepts

Planning what to write and how to present your information is important and I hope that you will do so when you plan the response to a question.

INTERNAL ASSESSMENT

Introduction

The internal assessment (IA) is compulsory for history HL and SL students. The IA, as it is usually referred to, is your opportunity to be the historian. You are given the opportunity to demonstrate the application of skills and knowledge to conduct a historical inquiry on a topic of your choice, without the time constraints of a written examination.

The IA is an investigation on any area/topic that interests you. However, the ten-year rule applies – any event that has taken place within ten years of your writing the IA cannot be considered. This is an individual activity – there is no group work allowed.

In a nutshell, you are a detective and a journalist. The IA teaches you valuable skills: research, which includes selection and evaluation of a range of source materials, communication, time management, editing of information, as well as the ability to reflect on the task once it is complete. You must be principled and acknowledge all your sources. The piece of work you produce has to be your very own.

How much time do you need?

The IA contributes 25% to the final assessment for SL students and 20% of the final assessment for HL students.

About 20 hours of teaching time is allocated to the completion of the IA. This time is used as follows:

- for the teacher to explain to you the requirements for the IA;

- as class time for you to work on the IA and clarify difficulties, if any, with the teacher;

- for individual consultation with your teacher as necessary;

- for the teacher to review progress and check for authenticity.

Therefore, once you understand the requirements of the IA, you should identify the topic that you wish to investigate and discuss it with your teacher. Your teacher will point out any ethical or confidentiality requirements. You will need to find the information required for the investigation and discard what is not relevant. Be sure that you have adequate sources to conduct your investigation.

Framing the research question

This is something that requires time and thought. The question should not be open-ended. It should be specific. This is because you can only use about 1300–1400 words to write up the investigation (section 2 of the IA). Broader questions are more relevant for the extended essay.

For example, consider the question "Was Germany responsible for the start of the First World War?" This requires a very detailed analysis, the question is unclear and quite open-ended. It's unlikely that you can do justice to it in an IA. On the other hand, a question such as "To what extent were General Douglas Haig's failures responsible for the tragedy of the Battle of the Somme in 1916?" is one that is limited in its scope. You can narrow your focus to General Haig and the Battle of the Somme.

What sort of sources should you look for?

From the material you study for paper 1, you are aware of the different types of sources. Sources include primary and secondary sources: books, letters, official documents, memoirs, oral history, interviews, documents, internet sources, to name just a few. It is important that you choose a range of sources to bring in different perspectives, to highlight the key concepts of causation, continuity, or change.

Once you have completed the first part of the task – research – you can move on to writing your investigation. The final stage is the reflection, where you comment on how you completed the task. How did you locate your sources? What were the challenges that you faced? You should also be reflecting on historical methods and challenges to historians, which you discovered during the process of completing your investigation.

There is an expectation that completion of the task includes 20 hours of teaching time, which includes directions from your teacher about the demands of the IA, mentoring what you do, providing some guidance on your research, and finally advice on your first draft. Some of this time may also be used to teach you the skills you will need – you should plan to have discussions with your teacher about your work. You are expected to work independently and to a deadline, set by your teacher. Your first draft will be looked at by your teacher who will comment on it and give you verbal and/or written advice, but will not edit it.

The internal assessment

It is a 2 200-word investigation.

- There are three parts to the IA:
  - Section 1: Identification and evaluation of sources
  - Section 2: Investigation
  - Section 3: Reflection

Possible choice of topics for investigation:

- A historical topic or theme
- A historical topic based on fieldwork – a visit to an archaeological dig, a battlefield, or a place of worship
- A local history study.

Possible questions for investigation:

1 What were the most important reasons for the failure of Operation Market Garden?

2 To what extent was the dropping of the atomic bombs on Hiroshima and Nagasaki a ploy to intimidate the USSR?

> **» Assessment tip**
>
> You should not rely only on sources found online. Examiners, that is your teacher and moderators, including the external IB moderator, will look at your bibliography to check on your sources. Do aim for a variety.

> **» Assessment tip**
>
> Two sources are required. Do choose sources that are different – one primary and one secondary, or sources that express divergent views.

>> **Assessment tip**

Do maintain a log to note down websites you have visited and books you have consulted. Do write down your thoughts and questions as you do your research. This is not a requirement, but it helps you to write the bibliography and respect the principles of academic honesty.

>> **Assessment tip**

Section 1 is to identify the topic and the question, as well as identifying two key sources.

Section 2 is *the investigation*, which includes a very short introduction, the body, and a conclusion.

Section 3 is primarily a reflection on the process and your thoughts about the study of history during the completion of the task.

>> **Assessment tip**

When evaluating your sources for this section and the investigation in general, be sure to do some research on the background of the creator of each source. Who is the person? What is his or her religious/ideological/political background? Why has this source been created? How reliable is it? For example, if one source is the account of a Rwanda genocide survivor, can the person be truly objective? Are newspapers reporting the event on the day truly objective, or are they selling a story?

The following table gives you a rough idea of how to frame the IA.

Section	Suggested word allocation	Associated assessment criteria	Marks
1. Identification and evaluation of sources	around 500	A. Identification and evaluation of sources	6 marks
2. Investigation	1 300 to 1 400	B. Investigation	15 marks
3. Reflection	around 400	C. Reflection	4 marks
Bibliography	Not applicable	Not applicable	Not applicable
Total (maximum word limit)	2 200 words		Total: 25 marks

Source: IB *history guide*

What does the word count not include? Bibliography and clear referencing of all sources is a *must*, but these are not a part of the word count.

Internal assessment criteria HL and SL

The IA is assessed against these three criteria:

Criteria	Marks
1. Identification and evaluation of sources	6
2. Investigation	15
3. Reflection	4
Total	25

Unpacking the criteria

Section 1: Identification and evaluation of sources

This is the section where you set up your investigation. Requirements for this section are as follows:

- The research question to be framed as a question.

- A brief explanation of the nature of the two sources that you have selected for detailed analysis. You will also need to make clear how these sources are *relevant* to the investigation.

- Analysis of two chosen sources in detail – this is where your paper 1 skills will be useful. You will analyse the sources in the same way – with reference to the *origin, purpose and content;* you are expected to *analyse the value and limitation* of these sources in relation to the investigation.

Section 2: Investigation

This section of the IA task is the actual historical investigation. Your work should be organized clearly and effectively. To do so you will need between 1 300 and 1 400 words. Do be sure to include detailed evidence and critical analysis that focus on the question you have asked. However, this is also where you will need your editing – especially paraphrasing – skills. Good editing helps you cut back on unnecessary details and focus on the key points you wish to make. The investigation should be coherent. Any claims you make must be backed by evidence, which is why it is so important to include your bibliography and reference your work.

Your conclusions must be included in this section. Any information that has been taken from your sources should be acknowledged, so do use footnotes or endnotes to indicate clearly where the information is from.

At the same time, avoid very detailed footnotes or endnotes. These should not be used to pack in information.

Illustrations, if used in the investigation, must contain captions and references to the source from which they are taken. An illustration should add to the investigation and not just make the investigation look pretty!

Section 3: Reflection

This is where you reflect on the task completed, on what the process has shown you about the methods and challenges involved in the study of history. You have to think like a historian. The role of the historian is to inquire, to find out, and to report. So what did you find out? How reliable were your sources? How did you decide which event was significant? You must be careful to relate your own experience to history as a discipline.

Some questions to consider when writing the reflection:

- What methods used by historians did you use in your investigation?

- How can the reliability of sources be evaluated?

- What is the role of the historian?

- Should terms such as *atrocity* be used when writing about history, or should value judgments be avoided?

Source: IB *history guide*

There are other questions in the subject guide for you to look at and use when you write up the reflection.

> **≫ Assessment tip**
>
> When choosing sources, avoid encyclopedias, dictionaries, revision guides, and revision websites. Your focus should be on academic sources: websites, books, academic journals, and so on.

> **≫ Assessment tip**
>
> Do ask your teacher to share with you copies of the subject report released after the examinations.

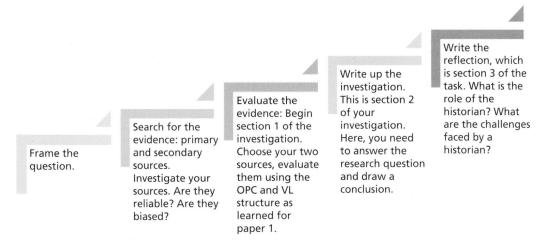

Frame the question.

Search for the evidence: primary and secondary sources. Investigate your sources. Are they reliable? Are they biased?

Evaluate the evidence: Begin section 1 of the investigation. Choose your two sources, evaluate them using the OPC and VL structure as learned for paper 1.

Write up the investigation. This is section 2 of your investigation. Here, you need to answer the research question and draw a conclusion.

Write the reflection, which is section 3 of the task. What is the role of the historian? What are the challenges faced by a historian?

▲ **Figure 1** An infographic to demonstrate how to write an effective historical investigation for internal assessment

Presentation of the internal assessment

When you have finished writing up the IA, it is time to give the presentation a little thought. There are no marks allotted for it, but good presentation always matters. A coversheet with the research question and the word count is ideal.

Here is a handy checklist:

- Include a coversheet with the research question and the word count.

- Make sure that each section is clearly identified.

- Section 1 – Have you included your research question? This is a requirement for section 1.

- Section 2 – Does your investigation answer your research question? Do you have a conclusion?

- Section 2 – Have you referenced your claims, using a recognized citation format such as MLA 2016 or APA Harvard? Referencing your claims is a requirement for this section.

- Section 3 – Have you completed your reflection? Is it a reflection of your task, methods used, challenges faced, and questions that may have arisen? Remember, in your reflection, there should be a clear connection between your experience as a candidate and the study of history as a whole. This is *not* solely about personal process – you will not achieve higher marks unless you do this. As mentioned earlier, there is information in the subject guide to help you further with this.

PRACTICE EXAM PAPERS

At this point, you will have re-familiarized yourself with the content from the topics of the IB history syllabus. Additionally, you will have picked up some key techniques and skills to refine your exam approach. It is now time to put these skills to the test. In this section you will find practice examination questions from papers 1, 2, and 3. Remember, although there is one question given here for each of paper 2 and 3, when you write paper 2 you will need to choose two questions each from a different topic; and when you write paper 3 you will have to choose any three questions. Additional guidance to these papers is available at www.oxfordsecondary.com/ib-prepared-support.

Paper 1

Prescribed subject 3: The move to global war

Read sources A to D and answer questions 1 to 4. The sources and questions relate to Case study 2: German and Italian expansion (1933–1940) – Causes of expansion – appeasement.

Source A   Editorial in the *Daily Express*, a British newspaper (30 September 1938).

Be glad in your hearts. Give thanks to your God. People of Britain, your children are safe. Your husbands and your sons will not march to war. Peace is a victory for all mankind. If we must have a victor, let us choose Chamberlain. For the Prime Minister's conquests are mighty and enduring – millions of happy homes and hearts relieved of their burden. To him the laurels. And now let us go back to our own affairs. We have had enough of those menaces, conjured up from the Continent to confuse us.

(Note: the phrase "to him the laurels" means to be satisfied with your achievements.)

Source B   Editorial in the *The Manchester Guardian*, a British newspaper (1 October 1938).

No one in this country who examines carefully the terms under which Hitler's troops begin their march into Czechoslovakia today can feel other than unhappy. Certainly the Czechs will hardly appreciate Mr. Chamberlain's phrase that it is "peace with honour."

If Germany's aim were the economic and financial destruction of Czechoslovakia the Munich agreement goes far to satisfy her. But, it may be urged, while the Czechs may suffer economically, they have the political protection of an international guarantee.

What is it worth? Will Britain and France (and Russia, though, of course, Russia was not even mentioned at Munich) come to the aid of an unarmed Czechoslovakia when they would not help her in her strength?

Politically Czechoslovakia is rendered helpless, with all that that means to the balance of forces in Eastern Europe, and Hitler will be able to advance again, when he chooses, with greatly increased power.

(Note: the phrase "rendered" means to have caused to become.)

Source C   Richard Overy and Andrew Wheatcroft, British historians, writing in the book *The Road to War* (1989).

In the end the question is not so much whether the Soviet Union really did make military preparations to help the Czechs, but whether a firm offer of Soviet help would really have made any difference. For the reality was that through the whole crisis Chamberlain was determined to keep the Soviet Union at arm's length. The Soviet offers of pacts, military talks, common fronts were never taken seriously, and in the end Chamberlain was instrumental in rejecting any Soviet participation in the Munich conference in which the Czechs were formally abandoned. The whole drift of Western strategy was towards accommodation of German demands to prepare the way for more rearmament and a negotiated general settlement at a future date. There was never a point at which a genuine offer of substantial military help from the Soviet side would have altered this strategy, while such an offer held all sorts of dangers if Soviet troops were once allowed to march westwards into Europe. . . Nor could Britain bring any real military strength to bear in the autumn of 1938; military discussions barely took place between Britain and France. The prospect of hard military planning with the Soviet Union was virtually out of the question.

Source D   David Low, a cartoonist, depicts the Munich Conference in the cartoon "What, no chair for me?" in the British newspaper *The Evening Standard* (30 September 1938).

WHAT, NO CHAIR FOR ME ?

1. (a) What, according to Source B, are the weaknesses of the
        Munich Agreement?   [3]

    (b) What does Source C suggest about why Britain signed
        the Munich Agreement?   [2]

2. With reference to its origin, purpose and content, analyse the
    value and limitations of Source A for a historian studying the Munich Agreement.   [4]

3. Compare and contrast what Sources B and C reveal about the Munich Agreement.   [6]

4. "Appeasement was a weak foreign policy and, when they adopted it, the British were more
    concerned about their domestic interests than stopping German expansion." Using the
    sources and your own knowledge, to what extent do you agree with this statement?   [9]

Paper 2

Topic 1: Society and economy (750–1400)

1. Evaluate the impact of famines and disease on the social structure of two states.

Topic 2: Causes and effects of medieval wars (750–1500)

2. Discuss the impact of two key individuals to the outcome of one war.

Topic 3: Dynasties and rulers (750–1500)

3. Evaluate the importance of the nobility in the governing of two states.

Topic 4: Societies in transition (1400–1700)

4. "Changing trade patterns were important to the development of modern societies." Discuss with reference to two states.

Topic 5: Early Modern states (1450–1789)

5. Compare and contrast the methods rulers used to maintain power in two Early Modern states, each from a different region.

Topic 6: Causes and effects of early modern wars (1500–1750)

6. Evaluate the religious causes of one early modern war.

Topic 7: Origins, development and impact of industrialization (1750–2005)

7. "Political stability was an important factor in the development of industrial societies." Discuss with reference to two states.

Topic 8: Independence movements (1800–2000)

8. To what extent have wars acted as a cause or catalyst for independence movements?

Topic 9: Emergence and development of democratic states (1848–2000)

9. Evaluate the significance of constitutions to the development of two democratic states.

Topic 10: Authoritarian states (20th century)

10. "The conditions in which authoritarian states emerged were mainly characterized by weak existing political systems." Discuss with reference to two authoritarian states, each from a different region.

Topic 11: Causes and effects of 20th-century wars

11. Examine the importance of economic factors in causing two 20th-century wars.

Topic 12: The Cold War: Superpower tensions and rivalries (20th century)

12. Examine the impact of containment policy on superpower relations between 1947 and 1979.

Paper 3 option 1: History of Africa and the Middle East

Section 8: European imperialism and the partition of Africa (1850–1900)

1. Evaluate the importance of economic factors in the European partition of Africa.

Section 11: 20th-century nationalist and independence movements in Africa

2. Discuss the role of the Mau Mau in Kenya's struggle for independence.

Section 13: War and change in the Middle East and North Africa 1914–1945

3. "The League of Nations Mandate system created problems for the mandatory powers." Discuss.

Paper 3 option 2: History of the Americas

Section 8: US Civil War: causes, course and effects (1840–1877)

1. Evaluate the impact of President Lincoln on the course of the US Civil War.

Section 10: Emergence of the Americas in global affairs (1880–1929)

2. Evaluate the reasons for US entry into the First World War.

Section 16: The Cold War and the Americas (1945–1981)

3. To what extent was President Kennedy's foreign policy successful?

Paper 3 option 3: History of Asia and Oceania

Section 11: Japan (1912–1990)

1. "Japan's foreign policy goals were not achieved at the Paris Peace Conference (1919)." Discuss.

Section 14: The People's Republic of China (1949–2005)

2. "The impacts of Great Leap Forward (Second Five-Year Plan) were mostly economic." Discuss.

Section 15: Cold War conflicts in Asia

3. "Military weakness was the main reason France lost the French Indo-China War (1946–1954)" To what extent do you agree with this statement?

Paper 3 option 4: History of Europe

Section 12: Imperial Russia, revolution and the establishment of the Soviet Union (1855–1924)

1. "The impacts of the New Economic Policy (NEP) were not only economic." Discuss.

Section 13: Europe and the First World War (1871–1918)

2. "The Alliance system meant that any small conflict in the Balkans would develop into a broader conflict." Discuss.

Section 14: European states in the inter-war years

3. Evaluate Hitler's economic policies during the period 1933 to 1939.